The Royal Canadian Mint and Canadian Coinage

STRIKING IMPRESSIONS

Printed in Canada

The Royal Canadian Mint and Canadian Coinage
STRIKING IMPRESSIONS

ISBN 0-660-11563-8

F72-8/1984E (DSS catalogue)

Contents

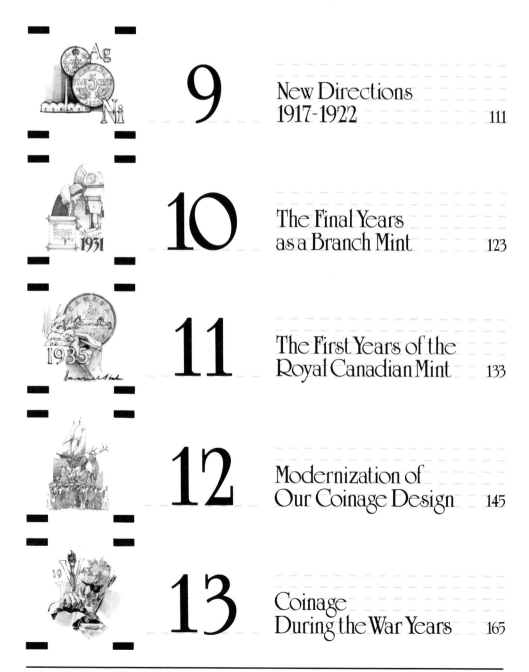

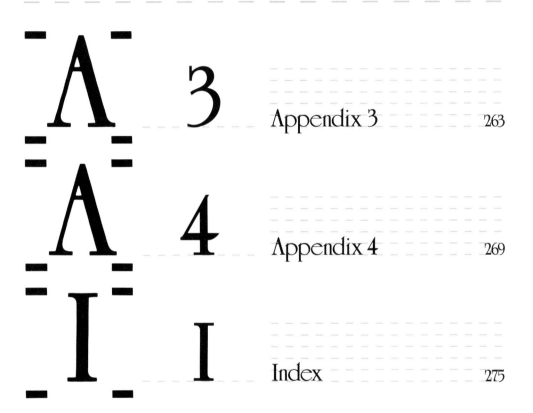

Foreword

The coins struck for circulation in Canada have been the subject of numerous books and catalogues. Unquestionably such books have made notable contributions to the high regard in which Canadian coins are held today.

During the tenure of my predecessor, Yvon Gariépy, an examination of these published works revealed that very few provided the history of our coinage and none recounted in detail the remarkable story of Canada's national Mint. Mr. Gariépy took great interest in satisfying this information need. It is therefore a privilege for me, as Master, to write the foreword for this book, and thus complete the series of events set in motion by my dedicated predecessor.

That "Striking Impressions" covers a period ending with 1983 is very appropriate, for this year marked the seventy-fifth anniversary of the Royal Canadian Mint. As with any major business anniversary, the passing of this milestone provides an occasion to reflect on the past accomplishments of former employees and to take renewed pride in our present work, while looking forward to the challenges and opportunities ahead.

Although this book is a history, it does more than recount events. It delves into those events to show how people blended old world minting traditions and contemporary technology to build a mint whose reputation for quality is world renowned. It is now, and I hope it always will be, a source of great pride for all of us in this organization to say, "I work for the Royal Canadian Mint".

J.C. Corkery

J.C. Corkery
Master of the Mint

Ottawa, December 1983

Acknowledgements

Special thanks is due to my associate, Terence Doyle, for his tireless assistance in the substantial task of collecting and editing the material for this history.

Special thanks is also due to the National Currency Collection, Bank of Canada, which allowed me to photograph many coins and tokens for use in this book.

Preface

Some worship it, others profess to loathe it, but few will deny that money is an important factor in modern society. The average person spends large amounts of time struggling to earn it in order to enjoy having and doing the things money can buy. Yet despite our preoccupation with money, many of us are almost totally unaware of how and where our coins and bank notes are produced, and what their history has been.

In Canada, our coins are produced by the Royal Canadian Mint. This institution, now a Crown Corporation, operates plants in Winnipeg (Manitoba), Ottawa (Ontario) and Hull (Quebec).

For many years, scattered information has been available to those interested in the Mint and Canadian coinage. This information, however, has primarily been in the form of catalogues which list the coins and their value to collectors, but provide only a limited historical commentary.

This book follows the opposite approach: it is not a catalogue, but an historical overview of the Royal Canadian Mint and incidentally of Canada's coinage. It takes us from the Spartan days of old Quebec to the Yukon gold fields and today's bustling city of Winnipeg. As the saga unfolds, we will see how in the space of 75 years our highly successful modern Mint evolved from a modest facility initially viewed by many as a colossal mistake. At the same time, we will learn how Canada came to have one of the most beautiful and respected coinages in the world.

James A. Haxby

Ottawa, December 1983

1

The Modern Mint

In Canada, coinage is big business.
It may be only a matter of pocket change
for any one individual, but for the Government of Canada, concerned with the shifting needs of over 25 million people, it is
an activity that requires substantial enterprise. Sometimes it yields great profit.

Profit normally derives from *seigniorage,*
the difference between the cost of making a coin and the "price" at which
the government sells it. At times the cost
for each dollar's worth of change has
been as little as twenty cents.

Under such favourable circumstances,
all that is needed for financial success
is a large demand . . . and Canada
has seldom been without that. Even
in the early unhurried days, requirements
were so great that, by the turn of this
century, there was already enough
coinage in the country to provide each
of Canada's six million people with more
than a dollar in change.

Today even that accomplishment seems
trivial. There is now over $1 billion
in small change in circulation: jingling
in pockets, making telephone connections, buying the latest news, deciding
which team "wins the toss" at the local
football game, or just sitting in dresser
drawers or in the collection boxes
of countless coin-operated machines.
Remarkably nearly all of this total has
been distributed since 1968. Most pre-
1968 issues have either been set aside
by collectors for their numismatic value,
officially withdrawn as worn or mutilated
or, in the case of some silver coins,
privately exported and melted for their
metal content.

Replacing the lost coins and answering increased demands due to economic growth, the government struck and issued to the public over one billion bronze, cupro-nickel and nickel coins in 1982 alone. Spread across the country, they almost disappear from sight, but at their point of origin on the Mint's shipping docks, they amounted to more than four million kilograms of metal. This is all the more remarkable when one considers that unlike most of our goods, from pencils to automobiles, these coins came from one institution, the Royal Canadian Mint.

The key to the Mint's success in achieving a sufficiently high output is modern technology, including powerful high-efficiency presses that can turn out coins at a rate of more than six per second. Even with the aid of advanced equipment in the Mint's plants at Ottawa, Hull and Winnipeg, nearly seven hundred employees work around the clock in three shifts to keep pace with the domestic and international coinage orders. They prepare the little disks we all carry around so nonchalantly.

The Ottawa plant.

Production of $100 gold coins,
Hull plant.
Alan Carruthers.

The Winnipeg plant. Henry Kalen.

"Every coin is the product of the lightning-fast action of the coining press..."

A coining press in operation,
Winnipeg plant.
Henry Kalen.

Every coin is the product of the lightning-fast action of the coining press in which highly sophisticated *dies* strike their designs into a shiny metal *planchette* or *blank*. Three dies form the design on any given coin: the *obverse die* (which bears the Royal portrait), the *reverse die* (the opposite side) and the *collar*, a plate with a hole in the centre which forms the coin's edge.

Obverse and reverse dies, collar, blanks and finished bronze cents, 1983.
Murray Mosher.

Pouring coinage bars,
Ottawa plant.
Alain Cornu.

Bronze coinage bar,
partly rolled strip and strip
rolled to final thickness
for producing cent blanks.
Murray Mosher.

A key to speedy production is the efficient preparation of the dies and the blanks they are to strike into coins. The production of blanks begins with melting the component metal(s) in crucibles placed in electric furnaces. Pure nickel is used for the 10-, 25-, 50-cent and one-dollar coins for circulation; however, most other coins require alloys of metals. The cent is bronze (copper, tin and zinc), the five cent is cupro-nickel (copper and nickel), the silver dollar for collectors is silver plus copper, and the $100 gold coin is a gold and silver combination. The molten metal is poured into molds and allowed to cool and solidify. The resulting slabs or bars of metal are passed repeatedly between powerful steel rollers, where the metal is squeezed into strips to the thickness of the coins into which they will be transformed. This also causes a considerable lengthening of the metal. For convenience of handling, the long strip is coiled.

Strip being fed into a blanking press,
Ottawa plant.
Murray Mosher.

6

"A key to speedy production..."

Blanks emerging from a blanking press
and being passed over a vibrating screen
for removal of defective blanks,
Ottawa plant.
Murray Mosher.

Scissel (scrap)
resulting from the blanking process,
Ottawa plant.

In the case of pure nickel coins, the Mint finds it more economical to buy the nickel strip from outside sources. Other strip is prepared "in house". When the strip is delivered to the blanking area, it is uncoiled and fed through straightening machines. The flattened strip is then run through high-speed *blanking presses* which punch out several blanks at a single blow. Incomplete blanks result when the punches partly overlap the strip ends. These are sorted out by vibrating the blanks on a screen which has holes just large enough to retain perfect blanks. The defective pieces, being smaller in diameter, fall through the screen into a collection box below. The defective blanks and the hole-riddled residue of the strips (collectively called *scissel*) are saved for melting and conversion into new strip.

At this point in the process, the blanks resemble common 'slugs' from electrical boxes. If the blanks are given raised edges and constant diameters, less force is needed to strike them into coins, and the coinage dies need to be replaced less often. The raised edge is imparted to the blanks by a machine which squeezes them between a revolving wheel and a stationary groove. In Mint vernacular, this process is called *edge marking* or *rimming*.

Working a metal tends to harden it, so the next step is to soften the blanks by *annealing*, a heat-treatment process. The blanks are heated and then allowed to cool in an atmosphere from which oxygen is excluded. The softened blanks are given a thorough washing, rinsed and passed through a drier to prepare them for striking.

Coinage dies are produced in the Ottawa and Winnipeg plants. This highly-specialized function begins in the Engraving Section in Ottawa. Each new design first comes into existence in the form of an artist's drawing. Some designs are generated by Royal Canadian Mint staff; others come from outside artists. In this form, the design receives government approval, after which the Mint proceeds with translation of the design into actual coins.

The exact steps involved in such a translation can vary somewhat, depending upon the nature and complexity of the design. It is best, therefore, to deal with a specific example, say, the $100 gold coin for 1983.

Edge marking (rimming) blanks, Ottawa plant.

Cent blanks before and after rimming.

"Each new design... comes into existence in the form of an artist's drawing."

Original artist's drawing
selected for the 1983 $100 coin.
Note the incorrect $1 denomination.

Revised artwork
(by Royal Canadian Mint staff)
for the 1983 $100 coin.

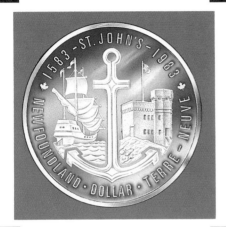 

Original negative model, in plaster,
for the 1983 $100 coin.
Murray Mosher.

Plaster positive model
for the 1983 $100 coin.
Murray Mosher.

Plaster negative model
for the 1983 $100 coin.
Murray Mosher.

For the reverse side of this coin, a flat plaster of Paris disc about 30 cm in diameter was prepared. Into this disc, the basic features of the ship, anchor and building were carved by hand. Fine details, such as the ship's windows and the stonework on the building, were omitted. This *original negative model* (its sunken elements exactly correspond to the raised areas on the coins-to-be) was placed face up in a shallow container and carefully covered with wet plaster. The dried plaster impression became a *plaster positive model*: its raised areas correspond to raised areas on the coins-to-be. The ship's windows and stonework on the building were added at this point.

A similar casting process, performed on the plaster positive model, produced the *plaster negative model*. With a final plaster in negative form, it only remained to generate a hard negative model in plastic. This was accomplished by making a rubber cast of the plaster negative model, giving a *rubber positive model*, and making an epoxy resin cast of the latter to produce an *epoxy negative model*.

For the obverse, the corresponding processes were unnecessary because a standard Royal portrait was already available in the form of an epoxy negative model.

Rubber positive model
for the 1983 $100 coin.
Murray Mosher.

The translation of the oversize models into coin-size tools proceeded via the *reducing machine*. In this wonderful device, one end of a long steel bar is mounted on a pivot point, and its other end is suspended from a connecting rod. A tracer attached to the bar is positioned so that it touches the centre of the three-dimensional epoxy model. Also attached to the bar is a cutting spindle. This cutter is mounted between the pivot point and the tracer (the exact position depends upon the reduction ratio desired) and is placed in contact with the centre of a brass disc. The machine is then started in motion. Both the epoxy model and the brass disc, which has a diameter of about 15 cm, revolve in a synchronized manner. At the same time, the tracer and the rapidly-revolving cutter are slowly lowered, so that their resulting path is a spiral. As the tracer follows the contours of the model, the cutter exactly duplicates its movements on a reduced scale. For the $100 coin, each cutting run (one for each side of the coin) required about thirty-five hours. Each *brass intermediate model* thus produced was then taken out of the reducing machine, for the addition of the rim beads and lettering.

Epoxy negative model
for the 1983 $100 coin.
Murray Mosher.

Brass intermediate model
for the 1983 $100 coin
before addition of lettering and beading.
Murray Mosher.

Brass intermediate model
for the 1983 $100 coin
after addition of lettering and beading.
Murray Mosher.

The next stage was a second reduction, which took the design on the intermediate model down to coin-size. The intermediate model became the pattern for the reducing machine's tracer to follow, and its design was copied into a steel block. After the machine had done its work, the steel block was touched up and hardened by heat treatment to become a *reduction matrix*.

A reducing machine in operation,
Ottawa plant.
The tracer is following the design
of the epoxy negative model,
while the cutter engraves the brass intermediate model.
Murray Mosher.

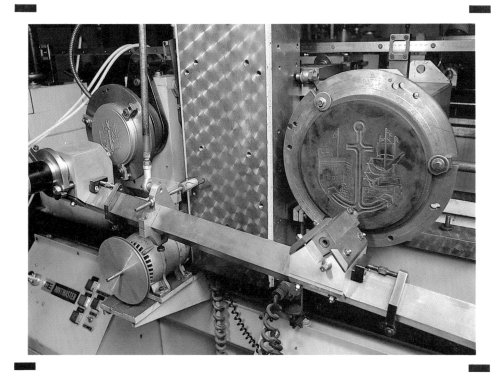

The *dies*, which actually struck the coins, were copies of the reduction matrices (one matrix for each side of the new coin). The matrix replication process involved the use of a powerful die-sinking press. Into this press was placed a soft steel cylinder, with its cone-shaped top touching the centre of the matrix. A single stroke from the press imparted the design of the matrix into the block below like the effect produced by pressing a signet ring into soft wax.

The resultant positive-design block, the *punch*, was heat-hardened for use in the final step. In an impression process similar to the above, the design of the punch was imparted to a series of steel blocks to provide the quantity of negative dies required for the coinage.

Reduction matrix, punch, die and struck example of the 1983 $100 coin.
Murray Mosher.

" This fundamental act, the striking of a blank with engraved dies, is the basis of minting."

Die making is often a less elaborate process for non-commemorative coins. Here, it is not necessary to generate a totally new design every year. Usually all that is required is a date change on the reverse. This is now accomplished by maintaining a set of partially-dated (currently 198-) intermediate *reverse punches*. Such punches are employed solely for making new matrices into which the final digit is carefully engraved by hand. From these fully-dated *working matrices* are made *working punches*, which make the dies.

In order to make the dies more durable and to impart a smoother, more brilliant finish to the coins, the die faces are given a thin plating of chromium.

This fundamental act, the striking of a blank with engraved dies, is the basis of minting. The Royal Canadian Mint is more than a mere production house: it also consists of an efficient administrative department, which is constantly solving problems and expanding marketing horizons. While it has seemed in the best interests of efficient production to diversify the Mint's plants, speed and quality are maintained by the centralization of its administrative facilities in a separate building located near the centre of Ottawa.

A typical example of the head office's involvement in solving coinage problems is seen in connection with the development of the current twelve-sided cent. Unlike many recent changes to our coinage, which have had an artistic origin (and affected most often the reverse designs), this rethinking of the one-cent came about because of cost factors, not appearance. As early as 1977, the price of the principal ingredient in the cent, copper, was high and seemed ready to rise higher. Required to pay market prices for its metals like any other business, the Mint was faced with the prospect of striking a product at an unacceptable loss unless it modified the composition or size. Given the number of coins involved, several hundred million, the loss could have been enormous. If the price of copper went sufficiently high to encourage the melting of the one-cent coins already in circulation, the situation could have been worse.

Some significant reduction in the amount of copper in the cent was obviously required. However necessary, this change could not be accomplished overnight. The main obstacle was the size of the cent's market: Canada's 25 million people. It was not a question of satisfying the specifications of merely a few hundred people or of only one or two groups. Every coin that goes into circulation and every significant change in the coinage has to meet the demands of everyone in the land.

" ... this latest innovation in Canada's circulating coinage was readily dropped into pockets and purses ... "

Round 1981 and twelve-sided 1982 cents.

Some demands were more precise and had greater weight than others. In particular, the Mint had to:

1. Create a coin which would neither activate nor unfairly jam existing vending machines

2. Develop a design which would continue to permit easy rolling and sorting by banks and other commercial bodies

3. Make the new cent easily distinguishable from other monetary objects, such as transportation tokens and, of course, the ten-cent piece

4. Produce an object which could be identified by touch, in response to growing recognition of the problems of the visually impaired

In addition to these considerations, the Mint had to recognize the usual inherent requirements of a coin: that the design be easy to strike, and that it wear well in daily handling.

Talks to define and later to fulfill these requirements began in 1977. They took place both "in-house" with design and technical staff and in the market place with the Toronto Transit Commission, the Halifax Bridge Commission and the Coinage Committee of the Canadian Automatic Merchandising Association. Radical alternatives such as substituting aluminum for bronze were considered and rejected.

Over the next three years, the formula for the present coin evolved: a diameter of 19 mm (down from 19.05 mm) and a thickness of 1.38 mm (down from 1.55 mm) was judged sufficient to maintain the individuality of the cent. This formula produced a coin which was lighter by some twenty-five percent than the cent first issued by the government more than sixty years ago. The 12 sides were decided upon to make it easier for the visually impaired to identify the denomination. Technical staff produced tokens with these specifications, and many pieces were tested in devices such as telephones and turnstiles as well as the Mint's own coining presses.

Formally announced to the public in late 1981 and distributed nationwide through the regular channels in early 1982, this latest innovation in Canada's circulating coinage was readily dropped into pockets and purses from the streets of Vancouver to the shores of Newfoundland.

How good was this solution? Certainly it could easily be coined and met consumer demands. But was much gained by the .17 mm reduction in thickness, and the small overall reduction in diameter? The answer lies in the nature of the coining business, where fractions make the difference. These small reductions save more than $1 million annually.

" What Ottawa is to coinage design and development, Winnipeg is to production."

Interior courtyard of the Winnipeg plant, with plaque.

Last year, nearly half of the new cents were struck in Winnipeg. What Ottawa is to coinage design and development, Winnipeg is to production. From the outside, the Winnipeg plant is too beautiful to be called a factory. Even inside there is a feeling of ease rather than labour, particularly in the areas designed for the public. Yet production figures indicate that this plant, one of the most modern mints in the world, means business. Operating 24 hours a day, often at full capacity, the production department can turn out over two billion coins per year.

Interior view of the Winnipeg plant.

Production equipment,
Winnipeg plant.
Henry Kalen.

Educational displays at the Winnipeg plant.
Henry Kalen.

"Canada produces millions of foreign coins annually..."

The Winnipeg plant is a key factor in the diversification of Mint activities. It is, for example, the centre for the Mint's burgeoning export trade. A formidable force in the world market, the Mint competes for orders against the British, American, Swiss and German mints. Canada produces millions of foreign coins annually, including such denominations as gourdes, centavos, agorot and poisha. These and many other pieces unfamiliar to Canadians are struck at the Mint for Israel, Nicaragua, the Cayman Islands and New Zealand, among other clients.

Foreign coins made by the Royal Canadian Mint.

"The Mint handles gold for most of the country's producers."

While not all of these coins require alloys that the Mint can prepare itself, they all play a part in the Mint's contribution to the export of Canadian metals. Among the most important of these metals is gold. The Mint handles gold for most of the country's producers. At its large Refinery in Ottawa, the Mint receives deposits from many Canadian mines as well as other scattered sources.

Each deposit is carefully melted in electric induction furnaces in order to produce uniform samples for assay. Then the combined stock is refined by chlorination and electrolytic processes to yield gold with a purity of .9999 from standard 400-oz. bars to granulated form. Silver is also produced as a by-product of the gold refining operations.

Electrolytic cells for refining gold, Ottawa plant.
Alain Cornu

James C. Corkery, present Master,
with Refinery products.
Murray Mosher.

Pouring silver bars in the Refinery,
Ottawa plant.

The primary use of gold by the Mint is for numismatic (collectors') coins and the bullion coins, the Gold Maple Leaf and its fractions. For this area of expertise, the Mint has its own world-renowned plant located in Hull. Opened in the 1960s to supply a rapidly increasing demand for numismatic coins, the Hull plant now deals in impressive volume for countries around the world. All numismatic coins are accorded the "white-glove" treatment. The preparation of both dies and metals is given special attention by the Ottawa plant. Then Hull takes over, striking each collectors' coin two or more times to produce a sharp image and dazzling finish.

Gold Maple Leaf $50 coins, Hull plant.
Alan Carruthers.

Proof set for collectors,
1983.

" ... the Mint produces several kinds of metallic objects that are not coins."

As another example of its broad activities, the Mint produces several kinds of metallic objects that are not coins. Medals have long been part of the Mint's repertoire. More recently, various tokens and trade dollars[1] for such events as the Calgary Stampede and Quebec Carnival have been added.

And yet, despite the Royal Canadian Mint's rapid pace and broad scope, its outstanding feature remains the high quality of its products. Its excellence in this area has gained the Mint an enviable worldwide reputation. Each of the billion-plus coins it now sends forth annually is a clear testimony to a careful combination of art and technology.

Medals struck by the Royal Canadian Mint.

This is the modern Mint of the 1980s.
But what was it like in earlier days?
What was the nature of the coinage
it produced? What coinage was used
by Canadians long before we even had
our own mint? The answers to these
questions take us back more than
300 years.

Trade dollars
produced by the Royal Canadian Mint.

2

Note:

[1] Trade dollars are special tokens, generally of $1 denomination, that are privately issued for profit. Typically they are emitted in connection with some civic event and are accepted at face value for a limited time by local merchants. Most are retained as souvenirs and collectors' items.

Colonial Canada Struggles for Coins

By the beginning of the 17th century when the city of Quebec was founded, nearly a thousand years had passed since the invention of paper money in China. But the now familiar bank note had achieved mixed success in the marketplace. People were hesitant to accept paper substitutes for their coveted coins. This is even more understandable when we recall that the larger denomination coins of the day tended to be "true value": they contained a quantity of precious metal equal in bullion value to the face value of the coins.

About a hundred years earlier, the status of coinage had been greatly enhanced when the Spanish came to the New World and gained control of vast supplies of gold and silver. Mints were set up in Mexico, Central America and South America. Soon gold "doubloons," silver "dollars" (also called "pieces of eight") and smaller denomination coins poured out in quantities the world had never seen before.

Even though Canada lay relatively near the Spanish-American mints, the coins usually went elsewhere. For over 250 years, Canada experienced directly a shortage of coins that Europe narrowly avoided. At times there were no coins at all, and frequently they were scarce.

The slow pace at which both coinage and minting were later to develop in Canada was partially determined during the country's earliest days by the interests of the first Europeans to arrive. Explorers and fishermen were

Spanish-America.
Gold 8 escudos
("doubloon"), 1773,
Mexico City Mint.

Spanish-America.
Silver 8 reales ("dollar"),
1747,
Mexico City Mint.

followed by fur traders who wanted to preserve the wilderness. They had little use for coinage.

Even when the first settlements were formed under the French, the need for coinage was not great. The colony of New France, situated along the St. Lawrence River, began under the control of monopolistic trading companies. Prices were set by the companies and payment was in goods. Thus traders used furs to purchase blankets, axes, rifles, beads, liquor and other supplies from the company store. These goods would then be traded to the Indians for more furs.

In 1645, the situation began to change. Local merchants gained control of the colony's trade and, with greater interest shown by the government of France, the population began to increase rapidly. The accompanying expansion in trade and commerce made coinage an absolute necessity.

The coins which came to the young colony were predominantly french. Since its founding, there had been shipments from the King. These coins were used to pay the colony's expenses; New France was financially dependent upon the mother country throughout its history. Spanish-American coins sometimes came through secret trade, but the circulation of all "foreign" coinage was officially frowned upon and was rarely legalized.

Jacques Cartier, 1491-1557.
Engraved by S. Freeman, 1850.
Public Archives Canada C-7298.

France.
Silver ecu, 1653,
Paris Mint.

"The coinage difficulties of New France were by no means unique."

The coinage difficulties of New France were by no means unique. In any colony with an unfavourable balance of trade, the meagre quantities of coins accumulated in the hands of merchants who periodically sent them back to the mother country to pay for fresh supplies of merchandise.

To make matters worse, the King's annual coinage shipment sometimes failed to arrive. All too often this was because none had been sent. France, though exceedingly prosperous for short periods during these years, was herself usually short of currency. Aside from domestic needs, there was a heavy drain on the treasury because of the wars in which France was frequently involved. Canada was not a major concern at such times.

Worst of all were the sinkings of the annual supply ships during treacherous transatlantic crossings. In the 1960s, the remains of one such wreck, *Le Chameau*, were found off the coast of Cape Breton Island. Still aboard was a large quantity of corroded silver *ecus* and untarnished gold *louis*, testimony to the great loss which hard-pressed New France suffered in 1725, the year the ship went down.

France.
Gold louis, 1680,
Paris Mint.

France.
Billon 30 deniers
("mousquetaire"), 1711,
Paris Mint.

France.
Billon 24 deniers
("sou marqué"), 1741,
Rouen Mint.

France.
Gold louis, 1723,
Paris Mint.

"When the King's ship arrived later, the card money was exchanged for coins."

In 1670, the French Government attempted to solve the colonial currency shortages by producing coinage[1] specifically for use in New France and other New World possessions. Unfortunately the special coins proved unpopular in New France for the very feature which made them unique: they would not be honoured in France. Though this guaranteed their stay in the colony, merchants disliked them because they could not be used to purchase supplies in the mother country.

Fifty-one years later, there was a second and final effort to provide a substitute for the Imperial coins, this time by a private company. This attempt proved no more successful than the first.[2] The population was left once again to struggle with the inconvenience of coin shortages.

The famous *card money* of New France was a response to such a shortage. In 1685, the colonial administrator, Jacques de Meulles, faced a desperate situation. The colony's troops were on the verge of starvation, and the arrival of the Imperial supply ship was months away. As a temporary expedient, he took playing cards, the only ready source of paper, and wrote promises to pay on the backs of whole cards or sections of them. When the King's ship arrived later, the card money was exchanged for coins. This practice was resorted to on later occasions, and eventually plain pieces of cardboard were substituted for playing cards.

French Colonies.
Silver 15 sols, 1670,
Paris Mint.

French Colonies.
Copper 9 deniers, 1721,
La Rochelle Mint.

New France.
Simulation of card money.
The text is translated, "Duplessi [signature]
For the sum of twelve livres 1714.
Vaudreuil. [signature] Bigon. [signature]."

New France.
Simulation of card money,
40 livres 1714.

Great Britain.
Copper halfpenny, 1770.

Great Britain.
Silver shilling,
1764.

Great Britain.
Gold guinea, 1775.

The British conquest of New France in 1763 marked the end of French power in this part of the world. It was, for the British, one more step in the extension of their influence over the entire region. Already they controlled the heavily populated and commercially active New England colonies, and mainland Nova Scotia which had been acquired from the French in 1713. Northward there was Newfoundland, British since 1583, and sprawling to the west, Rupert's Land, the wilderness area under the control of the Hudson's Bay Company.

The absorption of New France into the British colonial system did not lead by any means to one vast, integrated society on the continent. Nor did it immediately result in any marked improvement in the currency of the formerly French area. The residue of the French coinage accumulated over the last 120 years remained. Together with quantities of Spanish-American pieces from the allied English colonies to the south, these continued to be the basis for business dealings. British coins – guineas, shillings and halfpence – were slow to arrive in sufficient numbers. Even in Nova Scotia, the most firmly British of the later colonies, they were in such short supply that the government officially recognized the Spanish-American coins.

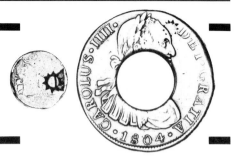

Prince Edward Island. Silver "plug" (shilling) and "holey dollar" (5 shillings) made from Spanish-American 8-reale coins.

After the American Revolution, significant changes occurred in Canada. British supporters, the United Empire Loyalists, journeyed north in large numbers. The existing population of some areas was literally overwhelmed. For the first time, Canada had a significant population including many people more accustomed to conventional business practices. Many of the new arrivals brought with them personal knowledge of the advantages of trade. They believed their new land had great potential. Among their other ambitions, the new citizens wanted a reliable source of coinage with which to develop some of that potential.

Unfortunetely for many years, Britain continued the disastrous policy of bimetallism: *both* the silver and gold coins were produced with a precious metal content approximately equal to the face value. Coins were struck mainly when private persons brought metal into the Royal Mint for that purpose. Very little silver was coined, and even less was exported during the last half of the 18th century. The official Mint ratio of values for the two metals undervalued silver, compared to the silver-gold ratio then prevailing in the marketplace. In these circumstances, most people who had silver bullion preferred to sell it for gold rather than take it to the Mint for conversion into coins. Even the few coins that were produced were too much needed in England to be shipped abroad.

As the shortage of small change grew worse, colonial governments began to clamor for special local coinages.

In Upper Canada in the 1790s, Governor Simcoe and the New Assembly devised a copper halfpenny for which dies were made and samples actually struck. It was only the Home government's disallowance directive that prevented the scheme from being fully carried out. A similar refusal thwarted the Nova Scotia government in 1817. The rule was clear: the British Government, like the French before it, was not in a position to provide sufficient quantities of Imperial coins for her colonies, but still would not allow the colonies to obtain their own from private sources.

Thus the expanding colonies were forced to an even greater dependence on foreign coins. By the early 19th century, these included not only the traditional French and Spanish varieties, but also coins from the newly-formed United States. A novel coinage arose in Prince Edward Island in 1813 when the governor ordered a limited quantity of Spanish "dollars" to be cut in a special way, creating a central "plug" and an outer ring or "holey dollar". The plugs passed as shillings and the rings became five-shilling pieces. Both were officially counterstamped, probably with a mark looking like a 10-pointed sun,[3] to make them legal.

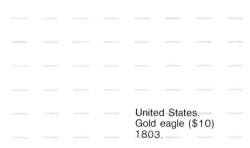

United States.
Gold eagle ($10)
1803.

The relatively new American coins, from the small denominations right through to the gold eagle ($10), were especially important for the future nature of Canada's coinage because they were based on a decimal system of dollars and cents. But for the time being, they only added to the commercial difficulties. Bookkeeping was clumsy because each foreign coin had to be assigned a rating in terms of the local pounds-shillings-pence system. The most famous rating was *Halifax currency* in which the Spanish-American dollar was equal to five shillings local currency.

Magdalen Islands.
Copper penny token, 1815.

The commercial pressure created by the War of 1812 brought the need for small change in the British North American colonies to crisis proportions. Merchants and traders solved the problem by smuggling privately-made coppers from the British Isles. These coppers were usually halfpennies and bore the word "TOKEN" to differentiate them from official coins.

British North America and Great Britain.
"TRADE & NAVIGATION" copper halfpenny token,
1812.

At first, merchants in Upper and Lower Canada tended to import tokens of an anonymous nature, bearing only the date and denomination, along with an inscription designed to encourage their use: "FOR THE CONVENIENCE OF TRADE"; "PURE COPPER PREFERABLE TO PAPER"; "SIR ISAAC BROCK HERO OF UPP^R & LOW^R CANADA." On the other hand, Nova Scotia merchants were bolder and placed their names on many token issues.

Upper Canada.
"Brock" copper
halfpenny token,
1816.

Nova Scotia.
W.A. & S. Black copper
halfpenny token,
1816.

Excessive issues of tokens led to stronger official condemnation; however, importations continued. In the late 1830s, the copper glut was aggravated by locally-produced pieces of poor quality, particularly in Lower Canada.

The answer to the copper problem in Nova Scotia was found through the issue of "official" tokens by the Provincial government. The pence and halfpence, produced between 1823 and 1843, were ordered without the knowledge or approval of the Home government. In Lower Canada, several Montreal banks resolved to issue good quality "bank sous" to drive the poor coppers from circulation. Eventually they succeeded.

In the meantime, the British Government was fighting a losing battle to reintroduce Imperial coinage into the British North American colonies. Bimetallism had been abandoned in 1816. Gold coins became the sole monetary standard, with silver coins reduced in precious metal content to become a subsidiary coinage. Silver and copper could now be struck at a profit to the Crown. A massive recoinage of silver began in 1816, followed in 1825 by copper.

Lower Canada.
Molson's copper sou, 1837.

Lower Canada.
Banque du Peuple "rebellion" copper sou token, 1837.

Lower Canada.
Typical "blacksmith" copper sou token, 1830s.

Nova Scotia. Provincial Government "thistle" copper halfpenny token, 1823.

Lower Canada.
Quebec Bank "habitant" copper sou token, 1837.

Great Britain.
Gold sovereign, 1817.

Great Britain.
Copper penny, 1826.

" But in North America it was virtually too late!"

Beginning in the 1820s, Britain was at last ready to supply her colonies with Imperial coinage.

But in North America, it was virtually too late. The mighty Spanish-American dollar and some of its subdivisions had become too well established. Besides the local pound (£ currency) and the British pound (£ sterling) had acquired different values, making circulation of Imperial coins difficult in British North America. For example, the ¹/₉ premium on sterling made a British shilling (12-penny piece) worth about one shilling and two pence in local currency. If someone bought an item for a shilling currency and paid for it with a British shilling, two pence change would have to be given.
On the other hand, there was no way to make change for a British halfpenny, also worth ¹/₉ more in local terms. Thus the circulation of sterling coppers was greatly impeded.

At the same time, the need for larger-denomination coins was being reduced. Various banks established from the late teens onward issued bank notes.

These forces combined to increase demand in the British North American colonies for special small-denomination coins valued in local currency, not sterling. During the 1820s to 1840s, the Home government was not prepared to agree to these requests so the copper tokens continued to fill the void.

Bytown and the Rideau Canal.
Lithograph by W.H. Bartlett,
1842.
Public Archives Canada C-2367.

Public Archives Canada C-20545.

By the 1850s, the Home government finally gave up the hope that its North American colonies would adopt Imperial coinage. It became more willing to allow local issues in the pounds-shillings-pence system. Copper bank tokens for Canada and penny and halfpenny coins for New Brunswick and Nova Scotia were all struck during this decade. The Nova Scotia coinage is particularly impressive. The Mayflower sprig on the reverse side is very beautiful, and the coins were struck in bronze instead of copper.[4]

Province of Canada.
Bank of Montreal copper penny token, 1842.

New Brunswick.
Provincial Government copper halfpenny, 1854.

Province of Canada.
Bank of Upper Canada copper halfpenny token, 1852.

Province of Canada.
Quebec Bank copper penny token, 1852.

Nova Scotia.
Provincial Government bronze penny, 1856.

As a result of increasing trade with the United States, however, the Province of Canada steadily pushed for coinage that would better fit the currency system of its southern neighbour. So in 1857, the first Canadian decimal coins — one-cent bronze, five-, ten- and twenty-cent silver pieces — were ordered from the Royal Mint in London. The reverse sides featured wreaths of leaves of sweet maple. The cent, with the leaves circling around in a serpentine fashion, has perhaps the most attractive design.

Two novel features of the Canadian decimal coinage proved to be a great mistake. The new cent was expected to be a convenient tool as a weight and measure: its diameter was one inch (25.4 mm) and 100 coins weighed exactly one pound avoirdupois. But this was largely lost on a public who preferred the much heavier and more familiar copper bank tokens. It would be the mid-1870s before the entire coinage of 9.7 million cents could be put into circulation.

Province of Canada. Provincial Government bronze cent and silver five, ten and twenty cents, 1858.

Crystal Palace, Toronto, 1858. Public Archives Canada C-1371.

"New Brunswick,
on the other hand,
did not want British silver."

The twenty-cent piece involved a somewhat different problem. It was easily
confused with the similar-size U.S.
twenty-five cent piece. In the 1860s,
when the latter became particularly
prominent, the problem grew worse.
The Canadian Government soon recognized its error, and from the 1870s
onward withdrew the twenty-cent
pieces. They were sent to England
for recoining into twenty-five cent
coins.

The other provinces were not long in fol-
lowing Canada's lead in adopting decimal
currency: Nova Scotia in 1859; New
Brunswick and British Columbia in 1860;
Newfoundland in 1864 and Prince
Edward Island in 1871.

Predictably enough, the colonial governments concentrated more on local pecu-
liarities than on establishing a coinage
acceptable throughout British North
America. The individual decimal currency
acts established dollars which sometimes differed from those of the neigh-
bouring provinces.

The Nova Scotian dollar was set at 1/5
of the British pound to allow easier circulation of Imperial silver coins in the province. Thus the florin (£ 1/10) passed as
a fifty-cent piece, the shilling was equal
to twenty-five cents and the sixpence
became a 12 1/2-cent piece in Nova
Scotian currency.

New Brunswick, on the other hand, did
not want British silver. On two occasions, it ordered its own silver five-, ten-
and twenty-cent coins, which were
struck in 1862 and 1864.

New Brunswick.
Provincial Government
bronze cent
and half cent,
1861,
and silver five,
ten and twenty cents,
1862.

Both Nova Scotia and New Brunswick also ordered bronze coinages. New Brunswick required only cents; however, Nova Scotia also ordered half-cents in order to have a coin to make change for the half-cent embodied in the six-pence. In a rare moment of confusion, the Royal Mint in London struck cents and half-cents for both provinces. The error was quickly discovered and most of the New Brunswick half-cents returned to the melting pot, but not before some of the unwanted coins had been mixed in with the Nova Scotia coins and sent to Halifax from where they slipped into circulation.[5]

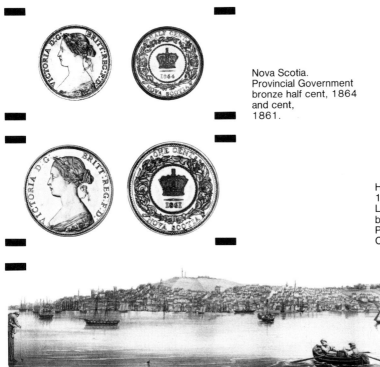

Nova Scotia.
Provincial Government
bronze half cent, 1864
and cent,
1861.

Halifax, Nova Scotia,
1860.
Lithograph
by Day & Son.
Public Archives Canada
C-11202.

Of all the British North American provinces, Newfoundland had the most extensive decimal coinage system. Its first coinage order was received in 1865 and consisted of one-, five-, ten- and twenty-cent pieces, as well as gold two-dollar coins. The two-dollar denomination was a compromise. The government originally considered a gold dollar similar to a coin issued in the United States, but chose the double value in order to obtain a coin not so likely to be lost by the heavily-dressed fishermen. This coin bore a triple expression of its value: two dollars, two hundred cents and one hundred pence. The latter referred to British pence, which in Newfoundland currency were exactly equal to two cents each. In 1870, the fifty-cent piece was added to Newfoundland's coinage system.

The designs employed for the reverses of the Newfoundland coinage departed radically from those for Canada, New Brunswick and Nova Scotia. The cent bears a wreath of the pitcher plant, the provincial flower. This interesting plant traps insects on its sticky leaves and uses them for food. The silver denominations carry arabesque designs on their reverses and the double dollar reverse consists mostly of the inscription and date.

Newfoundland.
Provincial Government
bronze cent, silver five,
ten and twenty cents,
1865,
fifty cents 1870 and
gold two dollars,
1865.

"The small beneath the great."

Prince Edward Island was the last province to initiate a decimal coinage. It received one-cent pieces in 1871 just two years before the province entered Confederation. The attractive design for the reverse side of this coin contains four oak trees — a mature tree sheltering three smaller trees at the left. The large tree represents Great Britain and the small trees symbolize the three counties on the island. Below is the Latin legend, "PARVA SUB INGENTI," or "The small beneath the great." Although the coins are not so marked, they were struck at Heaton's Mint in Birmingham, a private institution that coined on Imperial and colonial account when the Royal Mint was unable to handle all the work.

Prince Edward Island. Provincial Government bronze cent, 1871.

Province House, Charlottetown, P.E.I., 1880. Public Archives Canada C-73054.

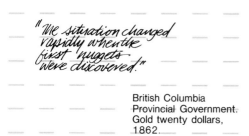

"The situation changed rapidly when the first nuggets were discovered."

British Columbia
Provincial Government.
Gold twenty dollars,
1862.

In 1858, about the time when Canada and the other colonies in the East were achieving the right to their own decimal coinages, gold was discovered in the Fraser Valley on the mainland adjacent to Vancouver Island. Britain had maintained a presence on the west coast since 1778, and the Hudson's Bay Company ran a large fur-trading network from its headquarters at Fort Vancouver on the Columbia River. Eventually the headquarters was moved north due to United States' claims on the land and the arrival of American settlers. The new centre for both Britain and the Company was Vancouver Island, which was made a colony in 1849. James Douglas, the head of the Company there, was made colonial Governor as well, since the majority of the white population was already under his control as employees of the company.

As in the East many years earlier, coinage was not a concern of the trappers and fur traders because they had little need for it.

The situation changed rapidly when the first nuggets were discovered. Shiploads of men streamed in from San Francisco, the nearest supply point. They disappeared into the wilderness on the previously unsettled mainland and returned months later anxious to exchange their golden booty for coin.

By this time, Douglas had already claimed the mainland (as the Crown Colony of British Columbia) for Britain, and, in August of 1858, he was confirmed Governor of this second colony as well. As part of the arrangements for the new colony, the British Government appointed a treasurer, Captain Driscoll Gossett. He arrived late in 1858,

Cameron "claim",
William's Creek, Cariboo, British Columbia.
Public Archives Canada C-19413.

"By the spring of 1862, the little mint was ready to operate."

carrying with him authorization to establish a mint in the colony, if necessary. Britain had recently benefited from a gold rush in Australia and was eager to take advantage of any further discoveries.

At first it seemed there would be no difficulty between Douglas and the ambitious Gossett. Douglas had been considering the possibility of establishing a mint at Victoria, on Vancouver Island, but a sudden lull in the gold finds relieved many of the coinage demands and most of the need for a mint. Soon it seemed that a simple assay office to determine the value of any gold brought in by prospectors was all that was needed.

But even this was unacceptable to Gossett. As Treasurer of British Columbia he needed facilities on the mainland, not at Victoria, if he was to serve any purpose at all. He managed to convince Douglas to establish the assay office on the mainland at New Westminster. Gossett hoped to have a large building which could be converted into a mint at the earliest opportunity. However, instead of the £3,400 he requested, Gossett received only £400, so he could only construct a very modest structure.

Even a small assay office would have proved excessive had it not been for the discovery of fresh gold deposits at the time the office opened in the summer of 1860.

Gradually the pressure for a mint and a local gold coinage began to mount

again. Many of the American miners had been involved in the California gold rush, when numerous private mints were set up and coinage was plentiful. For a time, Douglas continued to resist since the expense to the government would be $4 for every $1 coined. Finally in late 1861, Douglas approved the engraving in San Francisco of dies for $10 and $20 coins and the purchase of a small amount of equipment for coinage production.

By the spring of 1862, the little mint was ready to operate. The elated Gossett applied to Douglas for the title of "Deputy Master of the Mint." Governor Douglas, however, would not be pushed into opening the mint until he was convinced that the area's gold output was great enough to justify it. Furthermore there were labour problems. The assayers demanded an increase in pay if they were to be mint employees.

In the meantime a small number of $10 and $20 pieces were struck as samples, and some were sent to the 1862 International Exhibition in London. As a means of avoiding the expense of first refining the gold to a high degree of purity, the coins were made from only partially refined gold.

The following year, gold output began to fall again. This trend continued, and it was soon clear that the mint would never go into operation. When British Columbia (which had been combined with Vancouver Island to form a single colony in 1866) joined Confederation in 1871, the assay office was permanently closed.

3

Notes:

[1] The coinage consisted of a copper *double* (two-denier piece) and silver five- and twenty-sol pieces. For unknown reasons, the copper probably was produced in very small quantities and did not circulate in the New World.

[2] In 1721-22, the Company of the Indies shipped over 500,000 nine-denier copper coins to New France. These coins, with their legend "COLONIES FRANÇAISES", proved unpopular with the colonists because of their copper composition and size (over 25 mm); only about 8,000 could be put into circulation. The remainder of the shipment was returned to France in 1726, following an unsuccessful attempt to transfer them to the government of the colony.

[3] The attribution of this counterstamp is purely on the basis of circumstantial evidence. None of the official documents describe the counterstamp.

[4] The addition of a small amount of tin and zinc (a few percent) to copper renders sounder castings and a generally tougher metal that wears better in circulation.

[5] This explanation applies only to the currency strikes. The known proof pieces must be assumed to have fallen into public hands by other means.

Dominion Coinage from England

The Dominion of Canada, formed in 1867 by the union of the colonies of Canada East and Canada West, Nova Scotia and New Brunswick, inherited a less than ideal currency system. The circulating metallic money was a legacy of miscellaneous gold, silver and copper foreign coins, masses of unofficial and quasi-official copper tokens in sou, two-sou, halfpenny and penny denominations, and the official coins (mostly 1/2-, 1-, 5-, 10- and 20-cent pieces) issued by the colonial governments.

The presence of United States silver coins in 5-, 10-, 25- and 50-cent denominations presented a special problem. Lacking a sufficient coinage of their own, the citizens of British North America at first welcomed the American coins. Until the late 1840s, they had circulated freely but then disappeared when their value as bullion exceeded the face value. The situation reversed in 1853 when the U.S. Government began to issue 5- to 50-cent pieces with a reduced silver content. The new coins flowed north of the border where they enjoyed widespread acceptance at face value, even though their bullion value (and hence official exchange value) was somewhat less.

Sir John A. Macdonald, Prime Minister 1867-73, 1878-91. Photo taken in 1867. McCord Museum, Montreal.

Model of original Dominion Parliament Buildings, Ottawa. Public Archives Canada C-24.

After the U.S. Civil War began in 1861, the Federal Government in Washington introduced large quantities of paper money, most of it not redeemable in precious metals. Gold coins quickly rose to a substantial premium over both silver coins and paper money. It therefore became profitable to make large-scale exportations of U.S. silver coins to Canada. The exporters received payment in U.S. gold coin.

The Canadian purchasers of the U.S. silver were manufacturers, grain buyers and others who could pay out the coin at full face value for purchases and wages. When retailers and workers in whose hands the coins accumulated attempted to deposit it in their banks, they found they could do so only at a discount. Later the banks would not accept U.S. coins at all. Eventually it had to be sold to brokers, who renewed the cycle by selling it back to the manufacturers. This abusive system came to be called the 'U.S. silver nuisance.' It plagued Canadians throughout the 1860s, and was the first of a number of inconveniences created by U.S. coinage circulating in Canada.

At first, the full extent of the American silver problem of the 1860s was not realized. By the time the Dominion Government was formed, however, the situation was serious enough to warrant official action. In 1869, some $1 million in U.S. silver was collected and exported. Surprisingly the effect of this exportation was hardly noticed. Clearly the Canadian pool of U.S. coins was much larger than had been realized.

United States.
Reduced silver content half dime 1860, dime 1861, quarter 1853, and half dollar 1861.

"Weir met with Sir Francis Hincks, the Minister of Finance..."

In the late 1860s, William Weir, a Montreal businessman, became involved in exporting U.S. silver as a private enterprise. Armed with expertise in the collection and exportation of coins, Weir approached the Dominion Government in the hope of mounting a massive effort to end the American silver nuisance. Weir met with Sir Francis Hincks, the Minister of Finance, in January 1870. The government promptly made Weir its agent for exporting U.S. coins and through his efforts nearly $3 million in American silver was removed from circulation in Canada. In 1880, a group of grateful merchants presented him with a magnificent silver tea service embedded with numerous U.S. coins.

Sir Francis Hincks,
Minister of Finance 1869-73.
Photo taken November 1869.
Public Archives Canada PA-25467.

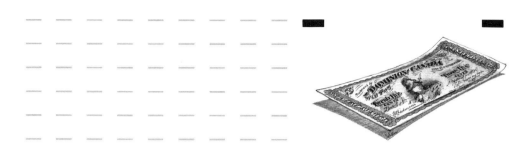

The other two aspects of the Canadian Government's plan for improving the silver currency were the procurement of a new Canadian silver coinage from England and a 'temporary' issue of 25¢ paper notes to fill the need for low-denomination currency while the government awaited the arrival of the Canadian coinage. The contract for engraving and printing the 25¢ notes, officially called 'fractionals' but more popularly known as 'shinplasters',[1] was given to the British American Bank Note Co. In quantities of $5 worth, the handsomely engraved notes could be exchanged for gold if the bearer so desired. By their gold-redeemable feature, the Canadian fractionals thus avoided the unpopularity of their U.S. cousins which were not redeemable.

First coinage for the Dominion:
silver five, ten, twenty-five
and fifty cents,
1870.

"Beginning in 1871 and continuing for some years, the Royal Mint was obliged to decline orders for Canadian coinages."

The initial printing of $500,000 worth of fractionals was in circulation by the end of 1870. The small notes became popular with the general public, and the government soon ceased to view them as a temporary expedient. Fractionals were issued up to the mid-1930s, serving as presents for young relatives, and as a handy way for mail-order houses to send 'change' to their customers.

The new Canadian coinage was obtained in England with the help of John (soon to be Sir John) Rose. He had been Minister of Finance from November 1867 to September 1869, and afterward joined a prominent banking house in London. His position there allowed him to serve as the Canadian Government's English agent and representative. He negotiated various trade agreements, arranged major loans and procured coinage.

Coinage needs were communicated to Rose, who then dealt with British Colonial Office Treasury officials to obtain authority and the minting. Rose also arranged for the silver bullion to be sent to the Mint, and for the completed coin to be shipped to its Canadian destinations.

Beginning in 1871 and continuing for some years, the Royal Mint was obliged to decline orders for Canadian coinages. Demands for Imperial coins taxed the Mint's outmoded equipment to the limit. Heaton's private mint in Birmingham was all too happy to take the business the Royal Mint could not

handle. Sir John Rose also made these arrangements.

The Heaton's Mint "H" mint mark on a ten cents, 1872.

All Dominion coins produced at Heaton's were from master tools provided by the Royal Mint. Sometimes, London provided the dies; other times, only punches were sent and the dies were sunk at Heaton's. In any case, all Heaton-produced Dominion silver coinage bore a tiny 'H' mint mark below the bow of the maple wreath on the reverse side.

To some extent, the designs for the new silver coinage were borrowed from the old Province of Canada coinage of 1858. The new federation and the former province shared 'Canada' as part of their name and this abbreviated form was used on the coins. It was thus possible to use the unmodified[2] 5- and 10-cent Provincial master tools for the Dominion coinage.

The tools for the 25- and 50-cent pieces had to be specially engraved, since these denominations had not been issued previously. The reverses are similar to those of the lower denominations; however, the obverses feature a diademed instead of a laureated portrait.

Between 1870 and 1875, some $3.2 million in silver coinage was produced for circulation in the Dominion, mostly in Ontario and Quebec. A commercial depression arose in 1875 and lasted for the next five years during which no further orders for silver were placed.

The copper currency also received Dominion government attention in 1870. This time the problem was not U.S. coins. It was the great number of token issues, some by provincial governments, some by banks, some by prominent individuals who preferred to remain anonymous. The coppers passed as halfpennies and pennies in the old currency system. None was legal tender, although the issue of most bank tokens had been authorized by legislation.

Handbill relating to the circulation of certain copper tokens as decimal coins, 1870.
National Currency Collection.

THE COPPER CURRENCY.

This has long been in such an unsatisfactory condition that a general desire for the substitution of cents for coppers was felt, and the Finance Minister, to meet this public requirement, has, by circular, authorized all Government Departments and Officers to receive the legally authorized coppers, sous and halfpence as cents, and pence as two cents, and has requested all bankers, merchants and others to do the same. All other coppers are illegal.

The following are fac-similes of the most widely-circulated coppers which are now to pass for cents; and all are requested to aid a reform so advantageous to the country as the substitution of the decimal currency throughout:—

TWO CENTS.   ONE CENT.   ONE CENT.   ONE CENT.   TWO CENTS.

The above cuts show the Bank tokens which will be current as cents after the first day of October, 1870. To these are to be added a few old Sous of the Bank of Montreal and La Banque du Peuple. Canadian and New Brunswick cents, and British half-pennies will continue current as cents, that being their legal value.

Montreal, October 1st, 1870.   WITNESS PRINT MONTREAL.

" In 1876, the Dominion applied...
for a fresh coinage
of bronze cents."

Recognizing the general popularity of the copper tokens, the government did not try to replace them for the time being. Instead the bank tokens were adapted for use as decimal coins (the halfpennies to pass as cents and the pennies to pass as two-cent pieces) and made legal tender to 25 cents for a single payment. Beginning October 1, 1870, they were accepted by government offices. All other tokens were refused, at any price.

The one-cent pieces issued by the Provinces of Canada and New Brunswick continued to be accepted at face value. In fact, the Dominion Government inherited millions of unissued Province of Canada cents. The last of these coins, which had always been somewhat unpopular because of their light weight, were finally issued in 1875.

In 1876, the Dominion applied through Sir John Rose to the British authorities for a fresh coinage of bronze cents. The government decided upon a heavier coin – the same weight as the old New Brunswick and Nova Scotia cents and the British halfpenny. The increased weight was achieved by striking a thicker coin. The reverse for the new cent was adapted from the 1858-59 Province of Canada reverse. There was some initial uncertainty regarding the obverse side. The existence of pattern coins suggests that the government considered using the Province of Canada obverse with the laureated bust of Victoria. In the end, however, a diademed portrait was chosen and a new obverse had to be engraved. The $40,000 cent coinage of 1876 was struck at Heaton's Mint, and proved sufficient for Canada's needs until the early 1880s.

First bronze coinage for the Dominion: one cent, 1876H.

As the young Dominion gradually matured, and business became more extensive and complex, the government decided that the informal status held by Sir John Rose was no longer sufficient. In the spring of 1880, the post of High Commissioner for Canada in England was established. First to occupy the position was Sir A.T. Galt. Rose continued as a consultant to Galt and his successor, Sir Charles Tupper, and retained some direct responsibilities for financial matters. From the latter part of 1880 onward, however, the High Commissioner replaced Rose in the business of procuring coinage.

By 1880, Canada's economy recovered enough that fresh supplies of coinage were required. Between 1880 and 1883, substantial quantities of bronze and silver Dominion coins were produced at Heaton's Mint. From 1884 onward, the Dominion coinages were almost always struck at the Royal Mint because its production capacity had recently been expanded by a major renovation.

Lord Strathcona (Donald Smith)
drives the last spike
to complete the transcontinental railroad,
November 1885.
Public Archives Canada C-3693.

"The coinage of 1907 was the last manufactured in England..."

The demand for coinage after 1879 was such that few years passed without production of 1- to 25-cent pieces, right up to 1907 the final year of English-produced Canadian coinage. The fifty-cent piece was another matter. Demand for that denomination was generally light prior to 1906, and its distribution was not spread evenly across the country. The Assistant Receiver General in Victoria received a far greater proportion of that denomination than the relative population would have suggested. In some years, such as 1890, the entire coinage of 50-cent pieces was destined for Victoria.

The coinage of 1907 was the last manufactured in England, because in 1908 the Ottawa branch of the Royal Mint began operations. The events that led to Canada finally having its own Mint began 17 years earlier in 1890, a few years before the beginning of the fabulous Klondike gold rush in the Yukon.

4

Notes:

[1] The derivation of the term 'shin-plaster,' in reference to the Dominion 25¢ notes of 1870 and later, seems to be either directly or indirectly related to U.S. issues. During the Revolutionary War, General Washington's troops stuffed the deflated paper money of the day into their stockings to help protect their shins from the chilly tempera-tures of the winter at Valley Forge. From this practice arose the expres-sion 'shinplaster' to characterize any low-value paper currency.

In British North America (particularly Lower Canada) during late 1830s, large quantities of low-denomination merchant's notes circulated; these too were dubbed 'shinplasters.' The resur-rection of the name for the 1870 Dominion notes stemmed from a recol-lection of the earlier Canadian experi-ence, from the term's continued use in the U.S. after the Revolutionary War, or from a combination of both.

[2] During the 1870 coinage, changes were made in the rim of both sides of the 5-cent coin. This had nothing to do with the fact that the coinage was for the Dominion; it was purely a technical improvement.

Agitation for a Canadian Mint

In 1890, twenty years after the production of the first coins for the new Dominion, the use of British production facilities had become a well-established tradition in the system of coinage supply. By this time, it might have been preferable to have the coins of the land made at a domestic facility, particularly in view of the gradual awakening of a sense of Canadian national identity. But no official steps were taken. In the eyes of the politicians, where the change in their pockets came from, was not important. The existing system was appealing because it required a minimum of effort on the part of Canada — a letter or two now and then, and arrangements for the purchase of the silver and copper bullion. The country's coinage orders came as required and the government made a profit by purchasing the finished coins at less than their face value.[1] The establishment of a mint in Canada looked as unlikely at the beginning of 1890 as it had in 1870. Yet only a decade later, the Canadian Government was to proclaim enthusiastically, with the support of the majority of the Canadian people, that the country's coins would be made at home.

The beginning of the chain of events which ended in government sponsorship of a plan for a domestic mint came in Canada's Parliament on the morning of March 4, 1890. During a landmark address on the desirability of both a domestic gold coinage and a mint, British Columbia Senator T.R. McInnes moved for the adoption of a resolution:

"Resolved as the opinion of this House that it is both desirable and expedient that the Government should immediately pass a coinage act and establish a mint."

It was no accident that the first official proposal for a Dominion mint came from British Columbia. Most of Canada's gold then came from that province, and its miners were growing increasingly unhappy. Every ounce they dug out of the ground had to be sent to the United States to be sold. Transportation from the remote mining districts was underdeveloped and expensive. Besides the basic shipping costs, there were insurance premiums and the costs for middlemen to do the handling. Although it is difficult to be precise about the amount of profit lost – whether it was 5 percent or 10 percent or even higher – such added expenses could not be recovered during selling. The buying price was fixed and was not affected by how much it cost the seller to transport his gold. The few facilities for the purchase of unrefined gold in the gold-producing districts were more a hindrance than a help. Since these facilities did not include the equipment for determining the quality of the nuggets or dust, the buyers invariably offered a low "safe" price which cheated the miners.

To the frustrated miners, it was clear that only one solution could provide any relief: the establishment of a Canadian market for their gold. It was also clear that no market, whether governmental or otherwise, would spring up on its own. Nobody would enter the gold fields to buy at a good price as long as there remained the extra expense of exporting the gold to the U.S. Obviously there had to be a domestic requirement for the product. The miners saw this coming about in the prospect of gold coins for Canada.

For them a gold coinage was a logical conclusion. Dealing with minerals on a day-to-day basis, they preferred coins to paper money. In addition, such a coinage would reduce cash shortages in the area. The only large denomination coins available in quantity were American gold pieces, and even these were usually in short supply. This was doubly exasperating since they contained the very metal the miners sent south.

If Canada was to have a gold coinage, it would also need a mint. After all, there would be little point in creating a market for producers if the metal still had to be sent out of the country to be coined.

Thus the idea of a Canadian mint arose once more in connection with gold mining, but this time it was not limited to the coinage of gold. It was proposed that the new mint would produce Canada's subsidiary coinage as well. This was not just an attempt to guarantee that the facilities would be fully occupied nor was it a logical conclusion. Rather it was a fundamental economic argument in support of the whole enterprise. At that time, there was no profit in coining gold because such coins contained an amount of precious metal equal in value to the face value of the coins. The mint's operating costs would be covered by profits on the sub-

"McInnes' proposal... contained economic elements disturbing to both the government and the banks."

sidiary silver and bronze coinage. These were the exciting ideas which had been developing gradually in British Columbia since the province entered Confederation. Yet however appealing the concept of a domestic mint might be, and notwithstanding McInnes' claim that "There is no country worthy of the name of a nation that is without its own gold coin," the hopes of the British Columbia miners were doomed for the time being.

Despite its achievements since becoming a nation, Canada was a troubled country. In the past, progress had been seriously jeopardized by linguistic and religious tensions in the East and by rebellions in the West. Now there was the further challenge of a slump in world trade that threatened important export markets and virtually halted the immigration which the vast land so badly needed.

At the same time, the Conservative government was desperately struggling to remain in office instead of developing new initiatives. The momentum which had carried it to power, twelve years earlier, was running out and, in particular, Sir John A. MacDonald, its main driving force, was rapidly declining in health.

Not only was McInnes' proposal ambitious for the times, but it also contained economic elements disturbing to both the government and the banks. Paper money was an important source of profit to both. The banks issued their own $5, $10, $20, $50 and $100 notes,[2] while the government issued its treasury notes, called Dominion notes, in denom-

inations of 25¢, $1, $2, $4, $50, $100, $500 and $1000. Both bank notes and Dominion notes were redeemable in gold coin (British or American), but people seldom chose this option and most of the gold remained in vaults. For practical purposes, gold corresponding to only 25 percent of the total note issues was held in reserve, so the other 75 percent amounted to an interest-free loan. On the other hand, gold would be coined at a loss to the government. Gold coins contained an amount of gold equal in bullion value to face value. The minting cost thus represented a loss. It is understandable that the banks and government were hesitant to introduce a coinage which was not only unprofitable, but could possibly drive a portion of their paper money out of circulation.

Furthermore in 1890, the McInnes proposal was very much a regional matter. Canada was yet to achieve prominence in mining. The whole undertaking of mining and minerals had an unfamiliar, almost unreal aspect to most people who were not directly involved. The great Caribou gold rush was some thirty years in the past. Gold mining continued in British Columbia and Nova Scotia and made a start in Manitoba, but colossal increases in Canadian gold output were still in the future. Gold mining was of little consequence to the economies of Ontario and Quebec, the centres of population and political power. Thus the motion was turned back without being seriously considered, after only the most cursory — and, in general, very critical — remarks by the Government leader in the Senate.

Front Street,
Dawson, Yukon Territory,
1899.
Public Archives Canada C-20894.

McInnes accepted the loss of his motion, but he did not accept defeat. He was back on the Senate floor pursuing his proposal the following year, but he was no more successful than he had been in 1890.

It was not until 1897 that McInnes again rose to champion the cause of a domestic gold coinage and a mint. By that time, some important and, to him, encouraging changes had taken place. The world trade picture had improved and the Liberals, under the inspiring leadership of Wilfrid Laurier, had swept into power in the election of 1896. Moreover McInnes and his supporters had become better informed on such relevant matters as costs of minting machinery and the possibilities for profit on the production of subsidiary coinage. He had even raised his proposal above the status of a regional issue by securing the support of over forty chambers of commerce from all across the country.

Despite all the favourable signs, McInnes again met defeat. The new government terminated debate with an abruptness, which made it clear that the principal objections remained.

It took the Klondike gold rush, which was only beginning at the time of McInnes' 1897 address, to bring the whole matter of Canadian minerals and mining before the public. The sight of a formerly poor man arriving in Seattle or San Francisco with sacks of gold had an undeniably compelling quality. Certainly the newspapers had no qualms about the matter: "Gold Dust by the Gallon!" and "Farmer Has Largest Nugget Yet!" were typical headlines proclaiming the biggest gold rush North America has ever known.

Virtually overnight, events in the Klondike turned McInnes' seven-year-old campaign from a dream failing for lack of supporters into a popular cause for which he was the spokesman. Now not only the miners but also merchants from all across the country complained about the lack of a domestic market for Canada's gold. As long as such a market was lacking, the miners would inevitably spend much of their wealth outside the country. Profit opportunities were being lost, particularly in Victoria and Vancouver.

In the 1899 session of Parliament, the mint proposition was again introduced, this time by W.W.B. McInnes (the son of T.R. McInnes) in the more appropriate forum of the House of Commons. At last the matter received lengthy and careful attention. Although the banks had softened their objections to a gold coinage, and the debate exposed the weakness of portions of the former opposition, the scheme still went down to defeat.

Prospectors panning for gold
in the Klondike,
ca. 1897.
Public Archives Canada C-16459.

"Fielding's claim ... must be viewed purely as a political ploy."

The Liberal government, like the Conservative government before it, seemed unwilling to act. The main fear was that a domestic gold coinage might interfere with what the Minister of Finance, William Stevens Fielding, called "the very perfect system of currency . . . in Canada." It was also anticipated that because of the small coinages involved, a Canadian mint would not be as profitable as the existing system.

The only bright note for the mint advocates was a tantalizing suggestion by Fielding that there might be a way in which the country could have a mint. It would involve the use of Canadian gold to coin British sovereigns (£1 gold pieces) rather than domestic gold coins in dollar denominations. The existing balance between Canada's paper and metallic currencies would be maintained and, with the whole of the British Empire as a market for the sovereigns, the mint would not be idle when there was no demand for domestic subsidiary coin.

In holding out hope for a mint, Fielding wisely made no promises. He knew that in order to coin sovereigns, the mint had to be a branch of the Royal Mint in London, and therefore closely linked to it. He also had a communication from Britain expressing reluctance to set up a branch mint in Canada. It was considered preferable for the Canadians, if they must have a mint, to operate it as a Canadian institution "without let or hindrance" from Britain.

Considering the facts of the situation, Fielding's claim that a branch mint in Canada was "not at all beyond the bounds of possibility" must be viewed purely as a political ploy. The failure of succeeding speakers to even ask for further details of the branch possibility suggests that the opposition considered it as such.

Thus the 1899 debates ended with the government still refusing to establish a mint, but suggesting that under certain conditions one might be possible in the future.

William Stevens Fielding,
Minister of Finance 1896-1911, 1921-25.
Photo taken in 1911.
Public Archives Canada 25973.

5

Notes:

1. For most of the 1870-1907 period, the Royal Mint charged a price that was the sum of the bullion cost and a fixed percentage of the face value of the coinage: three percent for silver and ten percent for bronze.

2. In the mid-nineteenth century, the banks derived about fifty percent of their profits from their notes in circulation. This share gradually declined (in favour of deposits) thereafter.

A Mint
for Canada

Perhaps the most incredible step in the sequence of events leading to the establishment of a Canadian mint took place in 1900. In an amazing reversal of policy, the government suddenly became the chief proponent of the mint scheme.

Several explanations for this transformation can easily be eliminated. Neither the government nor the economy had changed significantly. The Liberals continued in power and Fielding remained Minister of Finance. The economy while strong was not noticeably better than a year earlier. The Klondike still captured attention, but no new fields of note had been discovered, no new rushes begun. The change could not even be attributed to any new initiatives by the mint and gold-coinage advocates. Their vigour had not fallen off by any means, but they did not make any new formal attempts toward their goal.

Fielding's explanation of the government's reversal was that negotiations with the British government made it favourable to press on for a branch mint. Once again, his public statements do not fit the facts very well. If anything, the British government had grown even more opposed to the establishment of a branch mint in Canada. Although it was willing to accede to Canada's wishes, Britain pointedly suggested that the Canadians, once they had carefully considered the details of the situation, would surely drop the idea. Permission to mark the proposed Canadian sovereigns with the words "CANADIAN MINT" was refused, and it was further alleged that sovereigns produced in Canada were likely to be melted down once they arrived on Home shores. These were the "successful negotiations" which allowed the Canadian government to make its announcement!

John Mortimer Courtney,
Deputy Minister of Finance, 1878-1906.
Photo taken May 1907.
Public Archives Canada PA-804744.

For an explanation of both this discrepancy and the government's decision, it is necessary to look further: 1900 was an election year, and the mint announcement was made by Fielding in a campaign speech. When Fielding hinted to the House of Commons early in 1899 that a branch mint was possible, it is likely that he strongly doubted that the idea would ever, as he suggested, "bear fruit." His suggestion served an immediate political purpose. It allowed the government to escape from a popular debate without appearing to be unduly negative.

While such a tactic could relieve the government party from a delicate position in the House, it could not serve their purpose indefinitely. What was needed was a decline in the enthusiasm of the country for the Klondike and, consequently, for the mint and gold coinage issue as a solution to the problems it presented. Instead, in the months following the debate, the Gold Rush continued unabated. The population of Dawson doubled and then tripled, and the number of claims in the area and the quantity of gold removed both increased.

With an election coming up, the government shifted its position because public support for the idea had grown sufficiently (just as McInnes had predicted) to overcome the objections of the bankers.

In making his announcement, Fielding excluded any suggestion of this explanation by stressing the continuity of the government's conduct, but few, if any, were deceived. Noting that the Minister was frustratingly evasive about the date of the important negotiations, *The Citizen* of Ottawa charged that "In this, as in every other matter of public policy, the government has either been driven – or drifted – into action."

Whatever the basis for the government's decision, a series of activities which followed suggested that the country would very soon have its mint. Fielding himself thought it would be operational within two years, and his actions soon after the October campaign announcement seemed to guarantee this. His most important action was to send Deputy Finance Minister J.M. Courtney to London for talks with the Home authorities. He was instructed to arrange the establishment of a branch mint, as well as to draw up some rough plans for a building and an outline of the machinery needed.

" In the meantime, Fielding attempted to locate a site for the project."

In the meantime, Fielding attempted to locate a site for the project. His search was conducted with the utmost secrecy through a local firm of barristers, in order to conceal the fact that a decision had been taken to place the mint in the East rather than in the West. Not even the Home authorities were to be advised of this for the moment. When Britain asked for some indication of the site, Courtney replied that for the moment an answer was not "convenient." To some extent, this secrecy was necessary to prevent land speculation, but there was also a wish to delay the inevitable criticism from the West.

Fielding also secured funding for the maintenance of the facilities as the British required. Although the mint was to be a British branch, Canada was to bear the cost of running it as Australia had when branch mints were established in that country. This led to doubts about the wisdom of Fielding's arrangements, and was to become an increasingly controversial point in the years to come, but Parliament approved. In May 1901, the Ottawa Mint Act was passed for the specific purpose of providing annually, in advance, an annuity of $75,000.

The admission that the mint would be in Ottawa was made when it was decided that Nepean Point, across the Rideau Canal from the Parliament Buildings and fronting the Ottawa River, would be a suitable site.

Fielding later claimed that the title of the Act should have made clear to everyone that the government intended to place the mint in Ottawa. He resorted to this position only after it had been revealed that the West was to be overlooked. In the meantime, many assumed the title designated only where the Act had passed, not where the building would be. At least for the moment, it seemed that there would be a building somewhere. Besides the progress in Canada, the British Government had prepared the necessary legislation and was waiting only for the announcement of an opening date before having it passed.

It seemed this announcement would not be very far off when Fielding, bearing building plans which had been revised over the past months, asked the Home authorities to send someone over to supervise construction. This was a promising moment. While a branch mint was not as flattering to the national pride as a purely domestic mint, at least Canada's coinage would be produced within her own borders. There was also the prestige of producing the world-renowned British sovereigns from Canadian gold, with the benefit of the Royal Mint's experience and expertise.

But instead of the anticipated start of construction in early 1902, a series of setbacks began which would ultimately bring the project to the verge of extinction. First Britain discovered that Canadian officials had departed dangerously from the plans sketched by the Royal Mint. In particular, they had chosen to reverse the flow of materials through the building. Rectifying this error meant that tenders were not ready to be let again until the summer of 1902.

This was followed by an even more devastating event: Canada decided that the Nepean Point site was unsuitable. There were those who found it difficult to believe that a site which had been acceptable for more than a year was suddenly inappropriate. Chief among the skeptics was J. Israel Tarte who, as Minister of Public Works, had approved the site in the first place.

There was good reason to fear that this was not merely another delay, but was actually the beginning of the road to oblivion for the mint project. In the House of Commons the government's intentions were questioned. The government always answered that it meant to proceed, and that the rejection of the original site had been made reluctantly. Current delays were the result of great difficulties in locating an alternate site. But now two other factors were of at least equal importance: the government's ambivalence towards the project and the changed conditions in the country.

The government's true sentiments toward the mint project were embodied in the Finance Minister. Contrary to his public protestations, Fielding, who had mentioned the concept of a branch mint only in desperation, never changed from his initial reluctance. On the one hand, he was forging ahead with site studies and legislation; on the other, he was having doubts and holding back. This was evident in his plans for running the plant on the most modest possible scale. Although he was aware that an annuity of £15,000 (about $75,000) had proven inadequate thirty years earlier for the Melbourne Branch, he encouraged Courtney to try to make £10,000 suffice.

It is not hard to imagine the effect on the government's momentum when such half-heartedness encountered the strict demands of the British Civil Service. Fielding was forced to obtain parliamentary approval for an annuity, not of £10,000 but of £15,000, and still more if required. He also had to agree to pay substantial allowance and pensions to the British employees, even if the branch closed. Furthermore, besides giving in to Britain's expensive building plans, Canada was expected to provide a costly protective fence for the facilities, and possibly a residence within the grounds for the Deputy Master.

"And wait they did, until well into the year 1904."

The government's lack of enthusiasm was coupled with a decline in the output and notoriety of the Klondike. This decline began in 1901, too late for the government to avoid giving in to the popular wish for a mint but early enough to save them from actually having to construct a facility.

Another factor was the establishment of an assay office in Vancouver. Its purpose was to provide miners with an accurate and official assessment of the value of their "takings." Such an office had long been considered as an acceptable solution to the grievances of the gold producers. During the 1899 debates, Fielding had mentioned the possibility of establishing an assay office instead of a mint. However no official action was taken pending a decision regarding the mint itself. When this decision finally came in 1901, Fielding anticipated that an assay office to supply the mint would be set up in 1902. As it happened, the Department of the Interior, acting on behalf of the mining interests, independently opened an office in Vancouver, in July 1901.

The government was now free to stand aside and watch the effects of the assay office on the pressure for a mint. As long as it could continue to pacify the miners, and it could well do so as long as the decline in output continued, there might be no need to proceed with the construction of the mint. After all the election of 1900 had been won handily. The Liberals could afford to wait and see.

And wait they did, until well into the year 1904. But then, instead of giving up the idea forever, they finally pushed forward with their former resolution: the mint would be built after all. Perhaps it was only coincidental that 1904 was another election year. Certainly there were those skeptics who supposed that once again the Liberals were activated by political motives. One such cynic in the House noted that "the question had been dangling before the people and done service in two or three elections." In Vancouver, the government's candidate even went so far as to suggest to his riding that, if elected, he would bring the mint to his city after all.

Political promises notwithstanding, another Ottawa site was finally secured and the contract actually let. The completion date was set for January 1907.

"The opposition could not help wondering aloud why a mint was suddenly considered so vital..."

Unfortunately for the government, such progress did not meet with the popular acceptance which might have been expected a few years earlier. The failure to complete the mint when the momentum was high caused not only a loss of support for the project, but a decline in its usefulness as the gold production of the Klondike fell off. There was a sharp increase in building costs and, at the same time, an increase in the vehemence of the mint's opponents. The new location on Sussex Drive was on private land which had to be acquired at a cost of $21,000. During a debate on the government's appeal for $200,000 to pay the newly-appointed contractor, the opposition Conservatives taunted the Liberals with the very arguments the Liberals had used to defeat the early motions of McInnes. Even more embarrassing, government leaders found themselves forced to counter these taunts with the ideas they had scoffed at a few years earlier. The opposition could not help wondering aloud why a mint was suddenly considered so vital, after the Liberals had dragged their feet for years. And given the time elapsed, it was now proposed to review the whole question again, or at least to examine more closely the reason for a branch rather than a Canadian mint. But the government had determined its course and further debate was irrelevant because the Liberals held a strong majority. The necessary funds were finally allocated and construction began in June 1905.

In its haste to get the building underway, the government committed a remarkable blunder. It neglected to keep the Royal Mint in London informed that its latest branch was rapidly taking shape in Canada. In the end, it was Canada which was to suffer from this omission as it delayed the opening for almost a year. The oversight was not discovered until early 1906. Fielding, noting that the building would soon be roofed and ready for the installation of machinery by August, approached London for some help with the outfitting and in particular for the appointment of a superintendent. Unaware that work was well underway, the Royal Mint eventually repeated advice given in 1900, a reply totally inappropriate to the existing state of affairs. Fielding cabled back in dismay bringing the British up-to-date on developments and pleading for a prompt reply. Their second reply was no less disturbing. The British now seemed to think that the mint was ready to go into operation and that immediate preparations were being made for the appointment of all of the required staff. Canada could not accept such a step as it would mean paying salaries to men who could not possibly have any work to do for at least another year. Again Fielding cabled London explaining that all he wanted for the present was one man. This confusion ended shortly afterwards with the appointment of the first member of the staff, Mr. Arthur H.W. Cleave, as Superintendent, beginning September 1, 1906. Cleave had served at the Royal Mint in London.

Arthur H.W. Cleave,
Ottawa Mint Superintendent 1907-1919,
Deputy Master 1919-1925.

> *"As with the Royal Mint in London, the senior official at the Canadian Mint was designated the Deputy Master."*

This appointment, however, could do nothing to alleviate the previous neglect by the government of the question of machinery. They had done nothing about the matter since 1901 and thought the equipment could be delivered and adjusted in a matter of a month or two. In fact, Cleave could not arrange to have it shipped from England before April 1907.

With the building completed and the machinery en route, Britain fulfilled the additional staffing requirements without any difficulty. In June 1907, Dr. James Bonar, who had been on the Board of Civil Examiners in London since 1876, was appointed as the first Deputy Master. As with the Royal Mint in London, the senior official at the Canadian Mint was designated the Deputy Master.

Dr. James Bonar,
Ottawa Mint Deputy Master 1907-1919.
Photo taken June 1908.

Ottawa Mint "TRIAL RUN"
equipment adjustment bronze token,
1907.

The official opening date was postponed from January 1907 to November 9, 1907, but this time the mint was prevented from commencing operations on schedule by the lack of a fence. Since the earliest stages of planning, it had been understood that the mint must, for security reasons, be surrounded by a protective fence. Nevertheless, when Dr. Bonar arrived late in the summer of 1907 just two months before the opening date, there was no wall, fence or pickets of any kind. Since the mint could not open at all let alone on time, without a fence, Public Works pursued the quickest route to have it erected: they awarded the work, without tender, to the contractor who had built the mint. The enormous cost of the fence, which finally amounted to three times the original estimate, resulted in loud protests, particularly since the expense had been incurred without inviting competition. The reason given for this extraordinary practice, which was legally possible only in an emergency, was that the fence indeed constituted an emergency. The Minister of Public Works claimed it was "utterly unforeseen."

But neither lavish expense nor political expediency could produce a completed fence on time. Again the opening date was postponed, this time to January 1908. Even so Bonar was worried that the schedule could not be met. Only at the last moment was it evident that the mint could at long last open early in the new year.

In preparation for the opening, a pair of fifty-cent-size dies reading "OTTAWA MINT TRIAL RUN/NOVEMBER 1907" were engraved and a small number of bronze test pieces were struck from them. This allowed equipment adjustments without striking actual coins. The production of coins, bearing the effigy of Edward VII (King of England since 1902), could wait for opening day.

6

Ottawa Mint
prior to completion of the fence and guard lodge,
September 1907.
Public Archives Canada PA-42283.

Ottawa Mint
after erection of the fence and guard lodge.
Public Archives Canada PA-8974.

Settling In

January 2, 1908, was the historic date of the official opening of the Ottawa branch of the Royal Mint. The elite from the financial and political circles of Canada were present when Governor General Earl Grey activated the press to strike a fifty-cent piece, the Dominion's first domestically-produced coin. A few minutes later, the Countess of Grey completed the ceremony by striking the first bronze cent.

1908 cent mounted by private firm as a souvenir of the opening of the Ottawa Mint.

Neither Finance Minister Fielding nor Deputy Master Bonar, however, had much reason to feel festive. The Mint could not yet produce domestic gold coins or British gold sovereigns, the goal which had sustained much of the long struggle to obtain a mint. Still worse, trade had slackened in the wake of the financial crisis of 1907 in the United States. There was little demand for even those coins the Mint was able to produce. There were even signs of an *excess* of coins. Within days of the opening, the Bank of Montreal complained to the Finance Department that it was burdened with large stocks of surplus coin.

Staff of the Royal Mint,
Ottawa Branch,
June 1908.
Dr. Bonar is seated at the lower centre.

At the best of times, this situation would have been disappointing. But it came fast on the heels of two abnormally large orders placed by the Dominion with the Royal Mint. The first was prompted by the heavy demands of the boom year 1906, the second by Bonar's fear that the new Mint might be unable to begin production on schedule. The effect was catastrophic.

During the early years of the history of the Mint, coinage production was authorized by Order in Council. This was not an efficient procedure since the amounts of coin produced were often at odds with the totals specified. Sometimes the output exceeded the quota, and officials would then have to scramble to obtain the authority of additional Orders in Council.

An Order in Council passed two days after the official opening gave authorization for the production of a modest $280,000 in silver coins and $20,000 in bronze. But even this was too much. The general striking of silver coins began on February 19, 1908, but the Mint was very seldom fully engaged that year.

" For the two men the immediate purpose of both enterprises... was to provide work for the Mint. "

Setting up coining presses.
Public Archives Canada
PA-9646.

As early as June, Fielding was investigating the possibility of staff cuts. He could not justify the high initial cost of the Branch or its heavy operating expenses if it was not actually needed. He probably wished that he had delayed the opening even longer. Without denying the fact that many of his employees had little to do, Bonar energetically opposed any internal changes. He pointed out that even the London Mint had sustained long periods of inactivity.

Bonar's attitude is understandable. Slack demand allowed him to put the Mint into operation at a leisurely pace conducive to smooth running, and to proceed with arrangements for a refinery. But it was still a difficult time for him as well as for Fielding, and their mutual discomfort finally produced positive action in two crucial areas: the deportation of American silver and the withdrawal of worn and mutilated coins. For the two men, the immediate purpose of both enterprises long sought by various groups was to provide work for the Mint.

Ottawa Mint viewed from the south,
ca. 1908.

Cleaning fifty-cent blanks.
Public Archives Canada PA-9645.

> *"By 1906, the amount of U.S. silver in circulation had again reached an undesirable level."*

United States coins had formed a variable but significant proportion of the silver currency in the country since colonial times. They were often welcomed when coinage was scarce. However there were two circumstances under which U.S. coins were not welcome: when they were depreciated because of exchange difference and when, by sheer volume, they displaced Canadian currency from circulation and deprived the government of a source of profit.

In the late 1860s and early 1870s, the Dominion government first ordered the large-scale deportation of U.S. silver coins. The unwanted coins were exported by the millions, and their removal made possible the successful introduction of Dominion silver coins beginning in 1870.

By 1906, the amount of U.S. silver in circulation had again reached an undesirable level. This time the government entered into an agreement with the banks to provide a solution. The banks collected and forwarded U.S. coin to the office of the Bank of Montreal in New York. The Finance Department then reimbursed the banks with Canadian coin and also paid all express charges involved as well as a commission of $3/8$ percent to compensate for the time used by bank employees in sorting and packaging. As a consequence of this arrangement, over half a million dollars in U.S. silver was deported between March 1 and August 1, 1906. Then the movement stopped primarily because the term of the agreement had expired.

There had been some agitation to deport Newfoundland coin as well. That colony was separate from Canada, and had its own currency until 1949. However since there was at least as much Canadian coin at large in Newfoundland as there was Newfoundland coin in Canada, no deportation action was taken. The most serious problem was that Newfoundland insisted upon issuing 20-cent coins, which were too easily confused with 25-cent coins in Canada. Fielding's pleas that they abandon the 20-cent denomination were at first ignored and finally, politely but firmly refused.

It was not until the Mint was open – and idle – that the matter of foreign coins in Canada again received proper attention. In January 1908, T.C. Boville, the Deputy Minister of Finance, began inquiries into the amount of U.S. silver in circulation through his Assistant Receivers General in various cities. All indications were that it was high, ranging up to 75 percent of the silver currency in British Columbia, even though some institutions such as Eaton's department stores and the Toronto Street Railway were in the habit of deporting it. Again the government attempted to enlist the aid of the chartered banks in removing the unwanted silver from circulation, offering terms along the lines of the 1906 agreement. However the banks refused payment in Canadian coin because they were already holding large surplus stocks. Since the banks could neither lend out the bags of silver in the vaults, nor count them towards their reserve requirements (for which only Dominion notes or gold were acceptable), they naturally preferred to be paid for their U.S. coin in some more useful form.

Thomas Cooper Boville,
Deputy Minister of Finance,
1906-1920. Photo taken December 1910.
Public Archives Canada PA-133306.

While this stalemate persisted, the Mint could receive no relief from its idleness through the government's efforts to reduce the U.S. silver in circulation. A solution was not arrived at until January of the following year. The government agreed to terms acceptable to the banks, including the right to return surplus silver coin to the Assistant Receivers General. The move could not bring work to the Mint immediately, but the process had been started. By August, the deportation had begun in earnest. The sincerity of the Canadian Bankers' Association in backing the decision is clear in their October circular chastizing those banks which were still not making the effort to separate and send off the foreign money.

The second area of government activity would necessarily have a more immediate impact on the Mint. The melting of worn and mutilated coin, and subsequent recoinage, would provide work promptly.

By the beginning of the twentieth century, a significant portion of the Canadian coinage was worn or mutilated. The public began to exert pressure to improve the metallic currency, and their complaints were seconded by various boards of trade from St. John, N.B. to Vancouver. The government was unwilling to act, not just out of inertia, but because no legislation or procedures had ever been put in place to enable action to be taken. This oversight can easily be accounted for, because Canada was yet a young country, and its coinage had only just been in circulation long enough for the inevitable problem to arise. The oldest coins of the Dominion had been issued less than forty years earlier, although some remnants of previous provincial coinages were still in use.

Various ideas were offered for withdrawing the worn coins, including their redemption at face value less the shortage in weight and the expense of recoining them. But everyone agreed it was up to the government to take action. It was unfair, as well as illegal, to expect the people to sell them for their metal value, which after all was barely half the face value even of new coins.

" At first the government attempted to evade responsibility."

At first the government attempted to evade responsibility. But as the chorus of complaints grew louder, the government reluctantly decided to give Canada legislation for redemption of smooth coin. When the legislation was enacted, though, it did little to alleviate the problem. It merely released the pressure on the government and placed it instead on the banks. The Finance Department was obliged to redeem worn coin at face value, but the banks had to collect, package and present it.

As a consequence between 1901 and 1907, only $13,000 worth of worn coins was returned for redemption. Meanwhile the condition of the coinage, particularly silver, became more and more discreditable. In 1909, one company in Toronto protested that seventy percent of the 25-cent coins in circulation were worn smooth, and that its employees constantly objected to being paid in such money.

Finally with the Mint still working at far below capacity, a more equitable system was agreed upon between the government and the banks. By June 1909, a number of banks were authorizing all their branches to collect the worn coins and to issue new ones. The government was now willing to redeem mutilated coins at a twenty-five percent discount, even though it was illegal to deface coins. As a result, the Mint received $219,000 in worn or damaged coins between June and October alone.

Such self-generated minting activity was less necessary in 1909 than it had been in 1908, because a general improvement in business conditions brought a return of the demand for subsidiary coin. Bronze coins were the first to be requested in January 1909. By early May, the Mint's stock was sufficiently low to justify the first authorizing Order in Council since January of the previous year for $20,000 worth of cents. At this time, some need was felt for silver as well and, in late September, $275,000 was authorized by another Order in Council. For the next few months, new orders were passed with increasing frequency. In all the Mint had struck over nine million pieces by the year's end, nearly double the amount achieved in 1908. From then on, it could consider itself firmly established. The Mint had made a satisfactory though slow beginning of the production of Canada's subsidiary coins.

But where were those glittering domestic gold pieces to serve as tiny mementos of the national pride and ease the purchasing problems of the miners? And what had become of the promised Canadian sovereigns, the coins which were to pick up the slack when the Mint fell into the kind of lull it experienced its first year? After all the gold sovereign was the coin that made the Mint a British branch rather than a Canadian institution.

"The underlying problem was that the gold coins ... required refined gold."

The underlying problem was that the gold coins, whether British or Canadian, required refined gold. Although Canada had a gold rush and now a mint, there was no refinery in all the land capable of the complex and costly work of bringing rough gold up to coinage standards. It was a lamentable situation, partially attributable to both Britain and Canada. Perhaps the awkward communications of the time were the chief problem.

Britain did not feel it necessary to discuss refineries in any detail when Canada applied for a branch mint in 1900. The Royal Mint had no refinery since it bought its bullion ready for coining from private refiners. The British believed the Mint in Canada would want to make the same arrangements. It is understandable that they would think Canada, as a gold-producing country wanting to produce its own gold coinage as well as sovereigns, would have the same secondary facilities as Britain. Thus the first plans drawn up by the Royal Mint did not include a refinery (although there was the suggestion that ground be kept vacant in case one should be needed). Being new to the whole business, Canada either gave little thought to the quality of gold needed or assumed that the Vancouver Assay Office could produce it.

It was the task of the newly appointed Superintendent of the Ottawa Mint, A.H.W. Cleave, to correct this misconception when he arrived to assume his duties late in 1906, more than a year after construction of the Mint had begun. Immediately there was a flurry of activity and, by December 1, the government's Chief Architect, David Ewart, was in London reviewing the task with the Royal Mint. An alternative plan arose out of this meeting: the refinery could be built in Vancouver, and that city's Dominion Assay Office moved to Dawson in order to be close to the gold fields. But the government still favoured having the refinery in Ottawa and, for almost another year until late 1907, it conducted further feasibility studies regarding the transfer of rough gold from the West to the capital.

In the midst of these drawn-out investigations, the Royal Mint in London and its newly appointed Deputy Master in Canada, Dr. James Bonar, complicated the issue. They asked again the disturbing question of whether Canada really wanted to be bothered with coining gold. If Canada gave up this ambition there would be no need for a refinery, said Bonar, somewhat naively. He had noticed since coming to Canada that gold coins were not in great demand, but he had only slight familiarity with all the agitation of earlier years. And, of course, if Canada were not to have a gold coinage or sovereigns, what was the point of having a branch rather than a Canadian mint?

Detail of 'C' mint mark on Ottawa Mint gold sovereign, 1908.

Fielding, who cannot have liked such discussions very much, finally put his foot down. Canada, and preferably Ottawa, must have a refinery. In 1908, the Department of Public Works was commissioned to prepare plans for the proposed refinery. Bonar, believing that the facility would be built before year's end, contacted London to discuss the appointment of additional staff.

Nevertheless the government delayed the order to begin construction, because of growing concern that it had mistakenly lavished money on a coinage operation which now stood nearly idle. The Ottawa Mint had been designed to produce up to twenty million coins per year, including two million gold coins. But the initial demand for silver and bronze coinage was falling far short of expectations, and the gold situation was even more precarious. Even if all gold then produced in Canada were sent to Ottawa for coining, the Mint would just have enough to produce the hoped-for two million sovereigns per year. How much gold Ottawa would actually receive remained a major uncertainty.

Shipments of rough (unrefined) gold began to arrive at the Mint late in 1908. The amounts were small – only 219 Troy ounces by the end of that year. In the absence of a refinery, the gold was handed over to the Assay Department for treatment. The Chief Assayer, Ralph Pearson, had come from the Melbourne, Australia branch of the Royal Mint and possessed a good knowledge of gold processing. At first, he purified the gold by an electrolytic method similar to that planned for the new refinery. Enough gold was treated in 1908 to allow Bonar to strike a token quantity of 636 sovereigns from dies that had arrived from London before the Mint opened. The coins' appearance created considerable response of a generally favourable nature.

Gold sovereign 1908, Ottawa Mint.

Early in 1909, the Mint formulated and published regulations for the delivery of gold to the branch. Proclaimed January 6, 1909, these regulations set out such details as the hours of delivery, the quantities to be accepted, the charges to be levied for assaying and refining, and the procedure for payment of the depositor. Each depositor was to receive the equivalent of his deposit in gold coin, which at that time could only be sovereigns or half sovereigns, and the extra fractional amount in the form of a cheque. Half sovereigns were never requested or struck. It was soon found that most depositors desired payment for the entire amount in a cheque in Canadian dollars. This concession was granted after the Mint found that the sovereigns could easily be disposed of at the local banks.

Despite the fact that gold had begun to arrive at the Mint months earlier, it was not until February 1909 that Fielding actually requested from Parliament the $30,000 necessary for the new refinery. The Minister of Public Works noted that the facility was "urgently needed" — surely an understatement. Nevertheless it was July before tenders for the contract were invited. Certainly it is more than coincidental that the request for tenders came at the same time as the increased coinage demands and resulting activity at the Mint, as if the government simply did not care to commit themselves further until there was some evidence of success with the first venture.

With the start of construction in 1909 began the doomed race between the growing shipments of rough gold and the completion of a refinery to handle them. The Assay Department simply could not treat the gold fast enough to keep up with the influx. Since, as Bonar said, it would be "suicidal" for the future of the refinery to refuse to accept gold deposits, the Mint had to borrow money from the Department of Finance to pay for them. This was not a popular move in view of the earlier expenses for the project and the government's low cash balances. Yet it did not seem unduly risky since the government would eventually be repaid in gold coin and the refinery, a modest single-storey structure, was to be ready by May 1910. During 1909, the Mint managed to strike and issue over 16,000 sovereigns from gold refined in the Assay Department.

Domestic gold coinage remained in the early planning stages. Months after the Mint opened, not only had the master tools not been engraved, but designs had not even been chosen.

The desire for dollar gold coins had been part of the mint agitation ever since the beginning, sometimes attracting a greater, sometimes a lesser share of the enthusiasm. Naturally, as with any innovation, there were opponents. The bankers feared that a circulating gold coinage would reduce the amount of bank notes they could keep in circulation, thereby reducing profits. Others, without vested interests, were more supportive.

About the time Fielding was finally converted, however reluctantly, to the point of view that Canada should have a mint, he also determined that she should also have her own gold coinage. As early as February 1901, he sounded out the U.S. Treasury Secretary, Lyman Gage, on the possibility of having Canadian and U.S. gold coins made legal tender in both countries for mutual convenience. Gage was barely lukewarm to the proposal. He doubted whether Congress would pass the necessary legislation for "sentimental" reasons, and added that he felt a Canadian gold coinage was not really required since U.S. coins ought to serve quite as well.

All talk about a gold coinage ended for several years when progress towards a mint was stalled. It was not until late 1907 that the matter was taken up seriously once more. By this time, there was little disagreement about the denominations required: $2.50, $5, $10 and $20, as in the U.S. But there was little or no agreement on design.

Numerous suggestions for designs had been forwarded to the government over the years, clear evidence of the popularity of the question. They ranged all the way from an 1898 plan for the repetition of the current silver format to such imaginative proposals as one from the accountant in the office of the Winnipeg Assistant Receiver General. In 1900, he proposed a Canadian *beaver*[1] of "bold and active" appearance with seven stars to represent the seven provinces of the day.

It was Bonar at the Mint who made the first official steps late in 1907. Working with the Dominion Archivist, Dr. Arthur Doughty, he tried to obtain a result which was both original and technically feasible. Perhaps it was at his suggestion that Fielding communicated to the Royal Mint in the summer of 1908 that the Arms of Canada should be considered for the reverse design.

Further suggestions were solicited from the Paris Mint. An artist named Borrel devised the concept of a wreath formed of wheat and maple leaves surrounding the value of the coin. This idea did not excite much enthusiasm for the matter was apparently dropped at once. Next negotiations were entered into with Henri Dubois, also of Paris, the engraver of the 1908 Quebec Tercentenary medal. His designs were not, however, to the liking of Mr. Fielding. The minister also contacted E.E. Taché, the Assistant Commissioner of Lands and Forests for Quebec, who had designed the Tercentenary medal. Taché finally submitted a number of rather detailed designs a year and a half later. Many unsolicited designs were received from interested Canadians. These included some interesting designs by one S. Stohr of Hamilton, Ontario.

Proposed designs
for Canadian gold coinage,
1909.
By S. Stohr.

> *"The only design in which the government took any continuing interest was the original Coat of Arms proposal."*

The only design in which the government took any continuing interest was the original Coat of Arms proposal. A good deal of correspondence had taken place over some of the troublesome details such as which side of the coin was to carry the word "CANADA" and whether the King's effigy was to be crowned. Fielding's wish to have a crown surmounting the Coat of Arms on the reverse had to be abandoned to avoid overcrowding the coin. The $2.50 denomination had to be sacrificed because Fielding wanted the denominations spelled out in words. This fractional denomination would be very difficult to accommodate on a small coin. He also elected to shelve any further discussion of the $20 coin for the time being, and his subsequent failure to resume interest in it led to the abandonment of that denomination. Beyond this, Fielding made few decisions with the result that 1909 ended without final designs having been chosen.

It was the imminent (or so he thought) completion of the refinery, and the arrival of gold in Ottawa that finally prompted Fielding to pursue plans for the domestic gold coinage. There were only some small design changes which he was anxious to see made on the $5 and $10. Nevertheless, several months were required for the Royal Mint to reconcile the Finance Minister's preferences with what was technically possible.

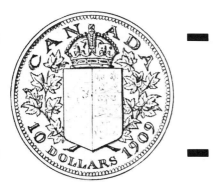

Royal Mint designs
for Canadian gold $2½ and $10, 1909.
Public Record Office, London.

7

Note:

[1] This suggestion was undoubtedly inspired by the fact that U.S. $10 gold coins were known officially as "eagles." By analogy to the U.S. terminology, the $5 piece was to be a half beaver and the $20 piece was to be a double beaver.

The End of an Era

By early April 1910, Canada seemed
to have arrived at the final stage
of its currency revision. The preliminary step of the Mint opening two years
earlier was about to be augmented
by the opening of the Refinery. In that
year, the country expected to be producing not only its subsidiary coinage as
it had in 1908 and 1909, but also silver
dollars and, more importantly, a domestic gold coinage and larger quantities
of sovereigns.

It was also the time during which a new
Currency Act was drawn up to formalize
all this progress. Under the Act, provision was made for the issue of $2.50,
$5, $10 and $20 gold coins even
though the Minister of Finance had
effectively abandoned the first and
shelved the last of these. The coins
were to be struck in .900 fine gold,
the remaining component being copper.
The weights were to be identical
to those of the corresponding U.S.
coins.[1]

King Edward VII.
Public Archives Canada C-31193.

King George V.
Public Archives Canada
C-31194.

Besides establishing a legal basis for a silver dollar issue, the 1910 Act also provided for a tiny increase in weight of the silver subsidiary coins. Previously the silver content had been calculated to bear the same ratio to face value as British silver coins. This led to some very untidy fractions.[2] Remedy allowances, or the margins by which the weight and fineness of coins were allowed to vary from standard specifications, were also fixed by the Act. Provision was made for the "Trial of the Pyx", an annual examination of randomly selected coins to ensure that they adhered to the legal specifications set forth for them.[3] After passage by Parliament, the Act was given Royal Assent on May 4. Amid such progress, who was to know that there was soon to be chaos?

One cause was the death of King Edward VII, on May 6, 1910. A new monarch meant months would have to be spent in the selection of new designs and preparation of new master tools for coinage obverses. The first ill effect of this additional work was the abandonment of hopes for the domestic gold and silver dollar coinages during 1910. The master tools for such new denominations could not be completed before those for existing denominations.

Since the King died in May, it seemed likely that the new obverses could be ready for use at the beginning of 1911. The need for new obverse punches did not threaten any immediate disruption of the existing coinage, for tradition permitted the use until the year's end of the dies portraying King Edward.

It soon became clear, however, that even seven months might not suffice. As early as the summer of 1910, Edward Rigg, Superintendent of the Operative Department at the Royal Mint in London, wrote to Bonar hinting at an unusually long delay caused by the lack of a modeller (one who works up large designs in plaster for reduction to coin-sized tools) and other critical staff at the Mint. Bonar moaned, "Oh, that Canada made her own dies for her own coins."[4]

Some hazards of delay he could guard against. Additional funds were secured from the Finance Department to purchase extra bullion, and domestic coinage stocks thought sufficient to see the Mint through to February 1911 were built up.

"The first break in the crisis came with the completion of the Refinery in January 1911."

Gold sovereign 1911,
Ottawa Mint.

At the same time, there was growing trouble on another front. Shipments of unrefined gold continued to stream into the Mint, but a series of delays in the construction of the refinery pushed the opening date back into 1911. This meant that there was only the Assay Department to cope with the 65,000 Troy ounces of gold deposited at the Mint during 1910. The Chief Assayer worked long into the night in an attempt to keep up. He even set up two makeshift furnaces to refine the gold by chlorination, a faster method than electrolysis. But the Ottawa Mint's gold debt continued to mount while the Finance Minister's alarm rose in proportion. The pressure on Bonar was enormous, as Fielding pleaded with him to repay the hundreds of thousands of dollars in badly needed funds[5] that the Department had advanced for payment of depositors. To make matters worse, the new King George V sovereign dies did not arrive as year's end approached. In his frustration, Bonar threatened to use the outmoded Edward VII dies, dated 1910, after the arrival of the new year.

The first break in the crisis came with the completion of the Refinery in January 1911. Ironically, there were still no dies available to commence striking now that the Mint had its Refinery. Finally on February 20, the new sovereign dies arrived and all necessary components were at hand. The Deputy Master promised Fielding that "Work will go on at a high pressure until we can begin consignments of coin for your department at regular intervals." Refinery workmen were called upon to work far into the night to hasten the reduction of the Mint's gold debt.

Electrolytic cells for purifying silver,
ca. 1911.
Public Archives Canada C-84435.

Gold was delivered to the Refinery in bars of unrefined or "rough" gold, which averaged 77½ percent gold, 12½ percent silver and 10 percent base metal. These rough bars were produced at the mine site in a process which required that vast quantities of ore be crushed to powder.[6] Three tons of ore would contain, perhaps, one ounce Troy of recoverable gold.

It was the work of the Refinery to bring the rough gold up to a purity of at least 99.5 percent (.995 fine) before it could be alloyed with copper to make .900 fine gold for coinage purposes. In the Refinery the rough gold was placed in electrolytic cells for purification.[7] The electrodeposited gold was melted into ingots and prepared for coining. The deposited silver, also melted into ingots, could either be used for coining or for refining more rough gold. The Refinery began operations with two silver cells and two gold cells supplemented by two more of each early in March. Bonar soon advised that another six of each be set up. The resultant annual capacity of the refinery was between 200,000 and 250,000 Troy ounces of fine gold. In all, some 90,000 Troy ounces came to the Mint during 1911 and a record number of over 256,000 sovereigns were coined.

With the gold crisis relieved, the focus of concern shifted to the subsidiary coinage. Coinage stockpiles originally planned only to last through February could not hold out much longer, but Bonar could not elicit even the promise of a delivery date for the new master tools for producing dies. He had cabled London desperately: "The delay may prove embarrasing." Instead the permission he had received earlier that the old 1910 dies could be used if necessary was repeated. As for the new dies, London replied coolly that Canada would hear "in due course."

Finally in early March, there was some tangible evidence of progress. The Finance Department was asked by the Royal Mint to choose between the two officially acceptable coin inscriptions. One gave the Royal Title in Latin, the other the English translation. Fielding's decision and reply were swift. He chose the Latin version, and it appeared that the master tools would arrive before the coinage stocks which Bonar had built up were exhausted.

" The Royal Title had been altered..." "

Near the midpoint of 1911, the first of the subsidiary coinage tools for the one cents were received. Unfortunately in eliminating one problem, they brought another which was to disturb all concerned. To the dismay of the Mint and Finance Department, the obverse was not as they anticipated. The Royal Title had been altered so that it lacked the abbreviation DEI GRA: (for DEI GRATIA), which was to indicate that King George V like his predecessors back to Richard III, ruled "by the grace of God."

For the Laurier government, the error could not have occured at a worse time. Another general election was only two months away, and the Liberals scarcely needed any new problems. They were already under pressure for their apparently indecisive attitude towards Great Britain, which was seeking to rally military backing in the face of anticipated problems in Europe prior to World War I. That situation was only aggravated by the appearance that Britain had, in this matter, acted without consulting Canada. Such action would have been in violation of the conventions under which the Mint had been established, which gave Canada control over domestic coinage designs (except where the Royal prerogative was concerned).

Obverses of bronze cents,
1911 and 1912,
showing original "Godless" legend
and addition of "DEI GRA:".

"Nevertheless, the Mint proceeded to strike and issue the new cents."

Nevertheless the Mint proceeded to strike and issue the new cents. They had not been keen to re-use the dies of the late King Edward. Now, more than a year after his death, this option seemed less appealing than ever. With coinage stocks badly depleted and the annual heavy summer demands so close, there could be no more delay. Thus, under pressure, the government altered the draft proclamations which had been prepared according to the correct inscription, and went ahead with approval of the design on June 30, 1911. During July the similarly objectionable tools for the remaining subsidiary coins finally arrived, and they too were given official approval.

Public consternation arose as these coins made their way into circulation. The government confidently advised the newspapers that the Royal Mint was responsible, and meanwhile diffidently approached that institution regarding its unprecedented action. The Canadians were expecting "good, sufficient and satisfactory" reasons for the change. They only hinted at their annoyance at the lack of consultation by mentioning the inconvenience created by the lack of a warning.

The answer they received in early September must have come as a severe jolt. Far from being unadvised of the offensive inscription, the Minister of Finance himself had approved it in reply to a letter from the Royal Mint in early March! Presumably in his haste to speed up the arrival of the tools, Fielding had failed to observe that all the inscriptions he was offered lacked the usual DEI GRATIA.

As for the reasons, the omission was nothing more than "an unfortunate oversight" on the part of the Deputy Master of the Royal Mint. He tendered his deep regret and promised the matter would be rectified for 1912. Meanwhile Canadians would have to live with the situation.

Whether the indignation aroused by the "Godless" coins had any part to play in the election which followed immediately is hard to say. In late September, after fifteen years of uninterrupted power, the Liberals went down to a crushing defeat.

For the ill-fated silver dollar still awaiting its introduction, this change of government was to prove crucial. Although the Liberals had not been ardent supporters of this denomination, they had allowed it to proceed towards the production stage during 1911. Various interested groups such as the Associated Boards of Trade of Eastern British Columbia had solicited a firm date for its production. However unsure they might be in private, the Liberals at least had not changed their minds publicly.

"The Mint anxiously pressed for permission to proceed with a coinage of silver dollars."

In 1910, the preparation for the denomination had reached the stage where a master matrix had been sunk for the reverse at least and from it a wax impression was made and sent to Canada for information purposes. In 1911, after the more urgent denominations were taken care of, the Royal Mint completed the necessary tools for Canada to produce its silver dollars. At least two pieces in silver were struck in London as "patterns." The initial obverse tools for this denomination were "Godless"; however, the known trial pieces all have the corrected legend.

In early November, a pair of matrices and two pairs of punches were delivered to Canada.[8] The Mint had acquired a new coining press just for the purpose of striking such a large coin. A trial striking in lead was presented to the new government for approval.[9] Although the government did ask the Governor General to approve the coin, its resolve faltered. The following day, Finance Minister William T. White told the Deputy Minister to let the matter remain on hold.

The Mint anxiously pressed for permission to proceed with a coinage of silver dollars. Finally, three days later, the facts were plainly stated in a letter from the Deputy Minister: "For the present it is not the intention of the government to give an order for this class of coin." The silver dollar project, at least for the moment, was shelved.

Matrix for reverse of silver dollar, 1910.
Printed backwards to appear as a coin would have looked.
Royal Mint, London.

Punch for obverse of silver dollar, 1911, with original "Godless" legend.
Royal Mint, London.

Pattern dollar, 1911.
Silver striking once owned by John Mackay-Clements;
the only known example in private hands.

Pattern dollar,
1911.
Lead striking.
National Currency Collection, Ottawa.

"The domestic coinage survived the delay better."

The domestic gold coinage survived the delay better. The basic reverse design was settled upon in 1910. It was the government's intention to proceed with the production of $5, $10 and $20 coins. Through an oversight, however, Fielding neglected to retract his December 1909 advice to temporarily set aside work on the $20. Thus, when the master tools were later ordered from London, Canada had to settle for the two smaller denominations.

Royal Mint designs
for Canadian gold $5, 1910.
Public Record Office, London.

"... it was clear that the coins would not be executed in 1911..."

The master tools for the $5 and $10,
dated 1911, arrived late in the autumn
after the Royal Mint had taken trial
impressions in gold from them.
As in the case of the silver dollar,
the delay in production had made possible the restoration of the contentious
words DEI GRA: in the obverse
legend.[10]

In October 1911, the designs were
submitted for approval, and this was
granted on November 8. But coinage
was deferred, because of the absence
from Ottawa first of the Minister
of Finance, and then of the Governor-
General. By early December, it was clear
that the coins would not be executed
in 1911 and would have to wait until
the following year.

Gold $5 and $10, 1911.
Photos of copper electrotypes
made from original matrices.

Notes:

1. If the Canadian coins had been proportional in weight to the sovereign instead, which was lightly overvalued at $4.86⅔ Canadian, the difference in intrinsic value between Canadian and U.S. gold coins would have been approximately one cent in every $500 worth in favour of the U.S. coins.

2. The Act increased the standard weight of the 50-cent piece from 179.3336 to 180 grains of sterling silver (.925 fine) with the lower denominations in proportion.

3. It is an interesting fact that the only 1908–09 Ottawa Mint coinages submitted to pyx trials were the sovereigns.

4. Bonar, of course, meant master tools (punches and matrices) when he used the term "dies." With the exception of those for the sovereign, the Ottawa Mint had always been capable of making its own dies once punches were at hand.

5. A total of $400,000 had been advanced from April through October of 1910 alone.

6. The gold in the powdered rock was then dissolved in sodium cyanide solution. The gold was recovered from solution by reduction with zinc and the precipitate melted and made into brick-shaped ingots.

7. This involved combination of the rough gold with about two and one-half times the amount of silver and casting into bars which served as anodes. The anodes would then be placed in silver cells, and the fine silver deposited. What remained of the anodes would be melted and cast into anodes again, placed in the gold cells, and the fine gold deposited. What remained of the anodes after the second deposition could be treated for the recovery of any other valuable metals.

8. The obverse tools bore the corrected legend.

9. This trial piece, undoubtedly produced in Ottawa, was stored away by the Canadian Government and forgotten. It was discovered in the late 1970s and was transferred to the Bank of Canada's National Currency Collection.

10. Here too, "Godless" obverse tools had already been made before the error was discovered.

The Refinery Becomes a Major Element in the Mint's Operations

The coinages of the period 1912 to 1916 were unremarkable, apart from the introduction of the domestic gold pieces.

In 1912 and 1913, the output totalled about 17 million coins per year. An industrial downturn caused production to drop to 11.5 million in 1914. The following year was even worse.

Wartime demands, however, were beginning to stimulate the national economy. Employment, wages, prices and the consequent demand for coins all rose sharply. After sinking to seven million pieces in 1915, production rebounded to over 19 million pieces in 1916, virtually the Mint's theoretical capacity.

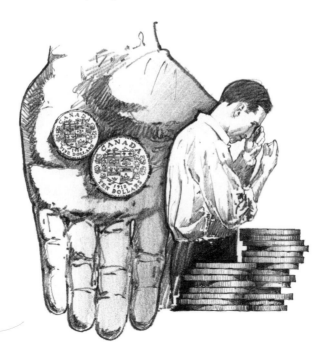

"...the new gold coins were not much wanted by the public."

Gold $5
1912.

With the year 1912 came the $5 and $10 gold pieces, finally expanding the Canadian coinage system to include high denomination coins. The Finance Department instructed Bonar in March to coin the first 8,000 of each denomination. By mid-July, the Mint had sent nearly $600,000 in Canadian gold to the Assistant Receivers General. After enjoying a brief popularity as curiosities, the new gold coins were not much wanted by the public. Most were destined for the Finance Department vaults in Ottawa, where they formed part of the gold reserve required for backing the Dominion notes. In fact, the majority of the 1912-14 $5 and $10 gold coins are still held for the government by the Bank of Canada!

Gold $10,
1912.

Examining and weighing coin,
1914.
Public Archives Canada PA-134857.

" ... the continued arrival of gold at Ottawa caused further difficulties."

Crown Chartered Mine,
Porcupine, Ontario,
1910.
Public Archives Canada PA-45234.

By the end of 1911, the Refinery had expanded its operations from two silver and two gold cells, to ten silver and twelve gold cells. But even this increased capacity soon proved to be inadequate. The electrolytic process was simply too slow to cope with the ever-increasing volume of gold bullion being sent in for refining. Not only was an unexpectedly high proportion of western gold being sent to Ottawa, but the output of the new Ontario mines was exceeding all predictions. When the quartz-based gold of the Porcupine field came on the market in 1912, it brought Ontario's share of Canadian gold production to 14 percent compared to only .4 percent the previous year. As the output of the older gold-producing areas of the Yukon, British Columbia and Nova Scotia tapered off, that of Ontario's Porcupine and Kirkland Lake fields steadily increased. They accounted for 66 percent of gold produced in Canada by 1919.

New Refinery regulations were published in 1913 to replace those set out in 1909. The fee schedule was revised, and depositors were given the option of payment either by cheque or by coin, rather than by coin only. This authorized what had already been a common practice since most depositors preferred and received cheques rather than payment in coin.

However the key to significant improvement remained the enlargement of the existing refining facilities. The Refinery improvements called for a second storey on the existing building and the introduction of the more efficient Miller chlorine method of gold refining. This process was first installed in Australia's Sydney Mint by F.B. Miller in 1867. It was proposed for use in Canada by the Mint's Chief Assayer, Ralph Pearson, after successful testing by the Assay Office.

In this method, a charge of approximately 650 ounces Troy of rough gold is melted in a fire-clay pot, and chlorine gas is injected into the molten mass. Chlorine attacks base metals and silver in preference to gold. The base metal chlorides and some silver chloride are converted to gases by the heat and go up the chimneys. They can be recovered by precipitation in the flues. The remaining silver chloride rises to the top of the molten mass in the pot and is skimmed off for further refinement. The refined gold which remains in the pot assays .995 fine or more.

" ... the output of the new Ontario mines was exceeding all predictions."

Unfortunately progress on the extension was slow. The $35,000 allocated for the project was not granted until June 1913 and the work was not completed until the end of 1914. The first chlorination took place in April 1915.

In the meantime, the continued arrival of gold at Ottawa caused further difficulties. Bonar was obliged to borrow more and more money from the Finance Department to pay the gold producers. In October 1913, the Mint's gold debt had soared to nearly two million dollars. To make matters worse, this increase came at a time when the government could ill afford additional expenditures.

At last the government had no choice but to slow down the inward flow of gold, and thus allow the Refinery time to process the backlog which had built up. In November, Bonar advertised that depositors would have to wait not the usual fourteen days, but "an indefinite time" for payment. Soon the gold was being sent to more efficient markets.

The following year saw momentous political and economic changes which would have a profound effect on Canadian gold and gold coinage. The First World War began in the summer of 1914. On August 22, in an attempt to gain control of the country's gold, the government passed The Finance Act. This legislation confirmed earlier orders in council which authorized banks to pay in their own notes rather than gold or Dominion notes, and suspended the redemption of Dominion notes in gold. The issue of gold coins or bars was prohibited by the government proclamation of September 5, although visitors to the Mint were still allowed to buy a few gold coins if they wished.

View of the Ottawa Mint from the southwest, showing the refinery after the addition of the second storey,
ca. 1915.
At the right is the Public Archives building, now the National War Museum.

The effect of these decisions upon the future of Canadian gold coinage was devastating. The major market for the $5 and $10 coins was the government, which had decided that gold bars were preferable for its purposes. The final blow came in January 1915 with the Finance Department's notification to Bonar that any outstanding orders for gold coins were cancelled and, henceforth, all payments to the Department were to be made with bars.

Chlorination furnaces in the renovated refinery, ca. 1915.
Public Archives Canada PA-134855.

Sovereigns were a somewhat different matter. The Canadian Government did not have the absolute control over them that it enjoyed for Canadian coins. As a branch of the Royal Mint, the Ottawa Mint had to allow those submitting gold for refining to exact payment in sovereigns. In practice, few depositors exercised that right. They preferred the convenience of cheques in Canadian dollars. Nevertheless the Canadian Government sought to control the issuing of sovereigns by stipulating that they be coined in future only on specific government order and not issued to the public. This inevitably brought the Finance Department into dispute with Royal Mint authorities in London. Poor Bonar, who was ever walking a tightrope between the two, was caught squarely in the middle.

Gold sovereign 1916,
Ottawa Mint.
Fewer than ten are known to exist today.

As long as it did not occur to the gold depositors to exercise their right to demand sovereigns, the conflict remained hypothetical. Out of more than $1.4 million in gold issued by the Mint in 1915, less than $600 of it was in coinage form, and no gold was coined at all that year. Almost the entire gold issue was acquired by the Finance Department in the form of bars.

The Canadian Government did not follow the example of Australia in overruling the Imperial order which permitted gold depositors to demand payment in sovereigns. The Finance Department finally agreed that the depositors were entitled to sovereigns provided they were willing to wait for their own gold to be coined. In 1916, a small coinage of sovereigns, 6,111 in number, was struck. Fewer than ten are known to exist today. Most of the original mintage apparently made its way to the U.S. Treasury where it was eventually melted down. As the war progressed, mine owners found they could escape an adverse exchange rate with the United States if they demanded sovereigns in payment for their gold. In the last years of the war, sovereigns began again to be coined in significant amounts, and the government's attempt to keep all the gold for itself was to some extent foiled.

In other matters involving gold, the government fared better. In September 1914, the Finance Department agreed to act as a trustee for the Bank of England to hold gold owed by the United States to Britain. With much of the world at war, shipments of such great value across the Atlantic were considered too risky.

In 1915, the situation was very different. Britain purchased much of her wartime needs from the United States, and the flow of gold was reversed. In September, the Bank of England asked for the assistance of the Ottawa Mint in refining large quantities of gold, most of which was to come from South Africa. The fine bars were then to be sent to New York to pay the debts of the British Government. The gold came to Canada because, handled discretely, it had a better chance of reaching Ottawa than of arriving in Britain. The first shipment of 1,100,000 ounces arrived in September and was refined within the allotted five months. Even with the reduced charges which had been set for the project, this was very good business for the Mint especially since the demand for subsidiary coin was low that year. However the Mint was kept too busy with the South African gold to deal with the output of Canadian mines. Complaints on this matter were handled evasively since the South African project was supposed to be kept top secret.

Having obtained a fifty percent increase in the Mint's annuity (to approximately $165,000) to meet increased manpower and material requirements, Bonar prepared for the next consignment of 1,500,000 ounces of gold from South Africa. Only one month went by before he found he had to submit a request for an altogether new Refinery to handle the expanding scale of operations. As he noted, all the improvements since 1911 had been piecemeal with the result that the facilities were ugly and inefficient. He suggested that land be used to the northeast of the Mint railings for a building containing fifteen chlorination furnaces. The existing Refinery would be converted to a storehouse.

But the government felt the Mint was too busy because of the war to tolerate major disruptions. Besides funds were short and the pressure was expected to diminish once the war ended. So the Mint had to settle for more temporary accommodations. The plans for these had to be revised yet again in July 1916, when Britain asked the Refinery to increase its output to one million ounces a month when called upon.

" This "temporary" structure..."

The Department of Public Works promptly constructed a plain brick building to the west of the original Refinery, just inside the main gates. This "temporary" structure, erected at the expense of the Bank of England, was built and producing refined gold bars in less than two months. Its equipment consisted of seventeen chlorination furnaces and two additional furnaces – one for holding molten rough gold ready for the chlorination furnaces and the other for keeping hot pots ready for replacement purposes.

Chlorination furnaces
in the "Temporary" refinery building,
1916.

Two new foremen were obtained from Australia to train the temporary Canadian staff, and additional assistant assayers arrived from England. At first, the new Refinery worked around the clock on three eight-hour shifts, six days a week. All premelting (for the purposes of assaying to establish the equivalent fine gold and silver content of the rough gold) was done in the Operative Department. By early 1917, it was possible to maintain the desired production rate of one million ounces of gold per month by working only two shifts per day. The staff had become more efficient with experience, and a large tilting furnace for pouring the fine gold bars had arrived.

Thus the Mint began what was to be a distinguished service to the British Empire and, at the same time, justified its existence in a wholly unexpected manner.

"Temporary" refinery building seen through the main gates at the southeast corner of the Mint, 1916.
Public Archives Canada C-37377.

9

New Directions 1917-1922

The final two years of the First World War were incredibly busy ones for the Mint. The Refinery received the final shipment of South African gold in June 1918. In all, a total of 19,492,359 ounces of rough gold were processed yielding 17,071,433 ounces of fine gold (then valued at over $350,000,000) along with 1,672,965 ounces of silver. The Bank of England was so pleased with the low refinery costs incurred that it offered generous bonuses to the workmen who had toiled long hours in the hot, poorly ventilated Refinery. But the gratuity was largely diverted into the pockets of Finance Department officials, and the dismay and bitterness of the Mint staff were understandable.

In addition to its regular duties and extra-ordinary Refinery work, the Mint's war-time service included the production of 11,389 dial-sights and 20,198 brackets of eyepieces for large guns under the guidance of the Superintendent, A.H.W. Cleave. It also turned out six million shilling blanks when the Royal Mint in London could not keep pace with demand.

Newfoundland. Bronze cent, 1917, Ottawa Mint.

The Ottawa Mint's coinage production was also impressive. The theoretical annual capacity of 20 million coins was far exceeded by means of a great deal of overtime work. Almost 29 million pieces were struck in 1917 and over 30 million in 1918. These totals included something new: coinages for Newfoundland and Jamaica. For the first time the Mint was striking non-Canadian coins other than sovereigns.

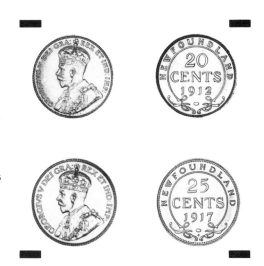

Jamaica. Cupro-nickel halfpenny, 1918, Ottawa Mint.

Still several decades from becoming the tenth Canadian province, Newfoundland had been accustomed to obtaining its coins from the Royal Mint in London. However, with the wartime pressure on the Royal Mint and the submarine menace to transatlantic shipping, it seemed logical to have Newfoundland's coinage made in Ottawa. This choice finally gave Canada the leverage it needed to convince Newfoundland to abandon its troublesome (to eastern Canadians) twenty-cent piece in favour of the twenty-five cents. In 1917, the one-, five-, ten-, twenty-five- and fifty-cent denominations were struck for Newfoundland on blanks identical to those used for the corresponding Canadian coins. These were about one percent lighter than the previous Newfoundland silver coins. The 1917 Newfoundland coins, which were given the "C" mint mark to show their Ottawa origin, made up about two million of the coins produced by the Ottawa Mint that year.

Newfoundland. Silver 20 cents, 1912, London Mint; and 25 cents, 1917, Ottawa Mint.

"Jamaica had turned to Canada for her coinage for essentially the same reasons as Newfoundland."

In 1918, only fifty-cent pieces were struck for Newfoundland, but in 1919, there was again an order for all denominations although in lesser quantities than in 1917. This was the last time that Newfoundland placed an order for denominations over ten cents. Only one cents were struck on behalf of the Government of Newfoundland in 1920.

The venture into non-domestic coinage was expanded with the addition of farthing, halfpenny and penny coins for Jamaica. This coinage, although consisting of less than 650,000 pieces, was in a way more important. The coins were cupro-nickel, an easier metal to work and strike than pure nickel. Cupro-nickel was a logical alloy for future domestic coins, and this provided an ideal opportunity for the Mint to gain experience in handling it.

Jamaica had turned to Canada for her coinage for essentially the same reasons as Newfoundland. However the Ottawa Mint was not equipped for the preparation of cupro-nickel blanks which were to be purchased ready-made from a firm in the United States. A delay was caused in coinage production by the fact that the American firm was fully engaged in munitions work. It was only through Canadian Government intervention that the blanks were obtained.

The 1918 Jamaican coinage was nevertheless executed to the complete satisfaction of colonial officials and quickly enough that a second order comprising almost a million pieces was placed the following year. The war was over, and metal supplies no longer presented any difficulty. Yet this order faced a greater obstacle than the first. Domestic demands, which took precedence over foreign orders, were running so high that the delivery date had to be postponed. In the end with a great deal of overtime work, this order too was satisfactorily completed. It brought the total number of pieces struck by the Mint in 1919 very close to 36 million, or 80 percent above the theoretical capacity. It was a staggering performance, especially for a facility which had produced barely six million pieces only four years earlier.

But the boom was not quite over yet: in 1920, over 42 million pieces were produced - a new record. By this time, the usefulness of the Mint was no longer in question. Secure in its efficiency, it now concerned itself with other more delicate matters.

The immediate postwar period was a time of dramatic and often turbulent change. The country was undergoing a major shift from an agrarian to an industrial economy. Inflation was rampant, and jobs had to be found for returning servicemen. Women received the franchise and the era of Prohibition was beginning. Violence erupted in the Winnipeg General Strike and Canadian nationalism was becoming a powerful force.

Change touched every area of national life, and the Mint did not escape. In 1919, Dr. Bonar retired to Great Britain. The right to choose Bonar's successor lay with Imperial Treasury Officials. However Arthur Cleave, former Superintendent of the Operative Department, was highly regarded by the Finance Department. This was undoubtedly a factor in his promotion to Deputy Master. John Roe, formerly the Accountant, became the new Superintendent.

The coining of Ottawa Mint sovereigns was suspended in 1919 never to be resumed. The Government was more anxious than ever to acquire all the country's gold production for its gold reserves to back the greatly expanded issue of Dominion notes. There had been increasing numbers of sovereigns struck in the years 1917, 1918 and 1919. These did not go into the gold reserves but were exported by the mining companies demanding them, notwithstanding the embargo on such export. The Government finally moved to buy up the whole gold production on advantageous terms. They paid in New York funds, then at a two or three percent premium. There was no longer any need for the mining companies to insist on sovereigns.

Fundamental changes were also in preparation for the nation's subsidiary coinage. Advocates of reform had long argued for the creation of a half-cent piece and a two-cent and a three-cent piece, and even a six-cent piece to be followed by the abolition of the five-cent. Others complained about the size of the coins: the cent was too large, the five cent was too small. Still others wanted to see the silver and bronze coins replaced with nickel, or to have bilingual inscriptions.

In the eager march of Canada towards the modern commerce of today, none of its coins was more out of place than the one-cent piece. It was too big for its declining buying power. The same inflation, which eroded the value of the coin in the marketplace, made it more expensive to produce so the profit earned by the government on the issue of cents decreased.

Even as decisions were being made to change to the small cent format, the composition of the existing large cent was being changed. The bronze alloy then used (copper: tin: bronze, 95:4:1) sometimes resulted in "blistered" blanks. As many as one in four of the blanks were rendered useless by this defect. Experiments revealed that the problem could be overcome by reducing the tin content of the alloy from four to three percent. Some of the 1919 and all of the 1920 large cents, including the cents struck for Newfoundland, were coined in the modified alloy.

" The coinage of Ottawa Mint sovereigns was suspended in 1919, never to be resumed."

The decision to reduce the size of the cent to conform more closely to its American counterpart was reached in March of 1919. Since the existing design, a garland of interlaced maple leaves, would not fit comfortably on the smaller coin, a new design had to be found. Finance Minister White asked the Ottawa Mint for sketch suggestions, but gave no specific guidelines apart from mentioning that he was personally fond of the old design. The Mint staff replied with some rather traditional ideas, none of which was considered suitable. Unexpectedly it was White himself who finally provided a useful plan. He proposed a simple design: two large maple leaves on either side of a large ONE. In the hands of Fred Lewis, a former Ottawa Mint employee, this idea was given four variations. In November, the Finance Department chose one of Lewis's sketches and placed the order for matrices and punches.

Initial production of the new coin was beset with difficulties. The obverse punch sent from England proved unsuitable. Dies made from it broke immediately upon application of the pressure necessary for striking coins. Valuable time was lost as the Ottawa Mint's engraver, using a portrait derived from a ten-cent punch, worked to produce a new matrix and punch. Meanwhile the demand for cents had reached an unprecedented level because of new taxes levied by the federal budget. The stockpile of the old large cents was running out. Finally the first small cents were officially released on April 15, 1920. The Mint poured out over 15 million of the popular small cents in 1920 to supplement the almost seven million large cents produced in the early months of the year.

Bronze cents:
original large version
and its smaller replacement,
1920.

The silver coinage was also altered, although not as noticeably, during this time of change. Silver was in great demand worldwide and quickly rose from its pre-war price of fifty cents per fine ounce Troy to near $1.40 by late 1919. This time, Canada's coinage profits were hurt far more significantly. The total profit on bronze coinage was less than $100,000 annually. But the five-, ten-, twenty-five- and fifty-cent pieces could easily yield a profit of over $750,000 when the silver price was favourable. Since it required less than one fine ounce to produce one dollar in silver coins, the government could make up to sixty-five cents on every dollar produced. Rising prices quickly cut this to ten cents or less.

For a short period, this loss was partially offset by increased demand for change. Parties in the United States seeing an opportunity for profit began to import Canadian coins. They melted them into bullion for sale to the Oriental market, all with the tacit approval of the Canadian Government. But by late November 1919, the price of silver was finally so high that this export business became a menace. Every dollar's worth of coins that was melted would now cost the government more than a dollar to replace.

Within days of the last critical price increase, the government acted under the broad powers of the War Measures Act. The silver content of the coins was reduced from 92.5 percent silver, or 925 fine (known as "sterling silver") to 80 percent or 800 fine silver, effective January 1, 1920. This enabled the Mint to continue to coin silver at a profit, which grew as the silver price began to subside.

Coincidental with this crisis was a renewed push for the use of nickel in Canada's coinage. Not only was it a fraction of the price of silver, but it was acknowledged worldwide as an excellent metal for coinage. Although Canada was the world's largest producer, suggestions for the use of nickel in coinage had always been disregarded. Finance Minister White now considered it as a replacement for the silver five-cent piece, after the American fashion.

The five-cent coin was the logical choice because many found the silver coin as troublesomely small as the cent was large. White, who was fond of the coin despite its size, declared that its smallness alone was not a sufficient reason to replace it.

The silver price increases of 1919 provided a more compelling reason. Despite its size, the five-cent piece accounted for more than one-third of all the silver used in 1918 and 1919 because of the large numbers struck. Estimates based on the then current high price of silver showed that a saving of about $150,000 annually could be realized by converting to a nickel coin.

"The five-cent coin was the logical choice"...

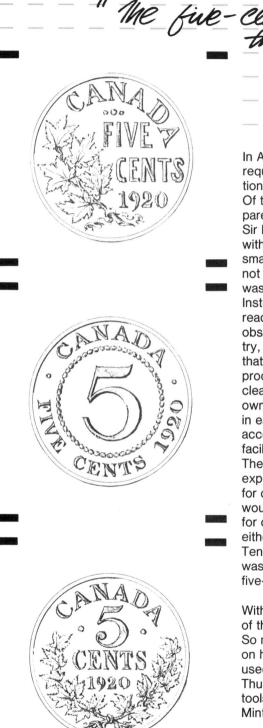

Rejected designs
for the nickel 5-cent piece,
1920.
Public Record Office, London.

In April 1919, design suggestions were requested from England with the intention of issuing the new coin in 1920. Of the four designs which were prepared, the Minister of Finance, now Sir Henry Drayton, chose the one with the greatest similarity to the new small cent. Although this decision was not taken until early in 1921, the delay was not caused by indecisiveness. Instead the supply of nickel blanks ready for coining had proved to be an obstacle. Pressed by the metals industry, the Finance Minister was determined that the coins should be an all-Canadian product. From the beginning, it had been clear that the Mint could not produce its own nickel coinage blanks, but only in early 1921 did the government accept the fact there was no Canadian facility capable of supplying their needs. The necessary equipment was too expensive to justify its installation solely for coinage purposes. Although the metal would come from Canada, the blanks for coinage would have to be produced either in England or the United States. Tenders were let and a firm in the U.S. was selected to supply the first nickel five-cent blanks.

With the problem of blanks out of the way, another difficulty arose. So many silver five-cent pieces were still on hand that they could not possibly be used up before the end of the year. Thus it was requested that the master tools being ordered from the London Mint should be dated 1922.

Early in 1922 with the new coins ready to enter circulation, there remained over three million of the obsolete five-cent pieces on hand. There seemed to be no demand for them so they were consigned to the melting pot. It now is clear that included in the melt was almost all of the 1921 coinage and a smaller portion of the 1920. Only a few hundred of the 1921s escaped, mostly those sold to visitors to the Mint during the year.

With the passing of the war and immediate postwar period, the frenzied activity of the Mint subsided. The record production of 1920 fell to 13 million pieces in 1921, and only 6 million in 1922. Due to the enormous quantities of silver coins struck in the previous few years and very depressed demand, no silver at all was coined in 1922 or for four years after. Bronze and nickel coins were still being produced, but the demand was light.

Foreign coinage contracts provided no relief. The Royal Mint in London was faced with the same drop in demand. It decreed that it, rather than any of the branch mints, should execute all coinages on behalf of governments not having their own mints. The Ottawa Mint was bound by the terms of its establishment to obey, and it yielded without protest. The Mint had entered the doldrums.

Silver five cents, 1921.
Most were melted
when the decision to change
to a nickel coin became official.

Nickel five cents,
1922.

The Final Years as a Branch Mint

The period between 1922 and late 1931 marked the Mint's last years as a branch of the Royal Mint. The transfer to full Canadian jurisdiction, when it finally came, was the result of a complex mixture of declining Mint activity and strained relations with the British authorities.

The demand for coinage was very slim from 1922 to 1926. Only one- and five-cent pieces were coined. Part of the demand for these denominations was created by "chain store" merchandising in which prices were set at one or two cents below even amounts. In 1925, the bleakest year, a mere 1.2 million coins were struck with a total face value of only $20,000. Interestingly the coins were not really needed for commerce; they were mostly struck to allow Mint visitors to see the coining presses in action.

Street promotion for Tip Top Tailors, Ottawa, 1920s.
Public Archives Canada PA-33971.

The larger denominations presented a worse problem. The demand for the twenty-five- and fifty-cent pieces was always less than for the lower denominations. Now it was negligible. In 1921, there were only $14,000 issued in twenty-five cents as opposed to more than $1,500,000 only two years before, and only $4,000 in fifty-cent pieces. Each year, matters grew worse instead of better until, in 1924, no coins in this latter denomination were issued. Stocks remained high and only the continuing need for one- and five-cent pieces, however slight, kept the coining plant from absolute inactivity. As in 1908, there were periodic attempts to reduce staff and costs since there was some doubt whether demand would resume for some time.

Finally in 1927-28, an upsurge in economic activity in the central provinces pushed up the demand for silver coins. Stocks of ten- and twenty-five-cent pieces were at last exhausted and needed to be replenished. Despite a slight renewal of requests for the fifty-cent denomination, it was recognized that the existing stock would be many years out of date before it could be taken up. Fearing that "old" dates on newly-issued coins would arouse the suspicion that they were counterfeit, the Deputy Master decided in 1929 to melt the coins and strike fresh supplies as needed. Thus almost half a million fifty-cent pieces dated 1920 and 1921 went into the melting pot. This turned the 1921 into a rarity, as only about seventy-five or so seem to have escaped destruction.

Ottawa Mint coins from the 1920s, including the rare 1921 50-cent piece.

It was during this inactivity that a second attempt was made to introduce a one-dollar coin. Although it failed, a completely redesigned regular coinage nearly resulted from the attempt.

The sixtieth anniversary of Confederation was approaching. In February 1927, Parliament passed an Act incorporating the National Committee for the Celebration of the Diamond Jubilee of Confederation. This emphasis on the Diamond Jubilee was caused by the fact that the fiftieth anniversary, or Golden Jubilee, fell in 1917 when the War made any extensive celebrations impossible. In addition to the more traditional celebration events, the Committee proposed the issue of a one-dollar silver commemorative coin to mark the occasion. There was some popular support for a commemorative piece, no doubt stimulated by the example of the silver 50 cents and gold $2.50 coins just issued by the United States to mark the 150th anniversary of the signing of the Declaration of Independence.

The idea was appealing but it was not to be realized. Time was short, and the Mint staff, after the experience of changing the one- and five-cent coins, knew that such things could not be accomplished quickly. Furthermore the Mint already had large stocks of unissued coins on hand, and a new silver dollar could not be justified economically. Pressure from mining interests continued, but the practical arguments against a new coin prevailed.

On the other hand, the inactivity at the Mint did seem to make this a good time to consider design changes in the existing coinage. The Deputy Master, while rejecting the introduction of a silver dollar, suggested that this was "a great opportunity to put into circulation coins of an artistic merit not hitherto evident in our issues." He could point to the example of the United Kingdom which was then in the process of reworking its coinage designs. The result was more aesthetically pleasing and easier to strike in the coining presses.

Thus inspired, the Mint arranged a design competition. Contest rules were sent out in May 1927. All qualified Canadian artists were invited to submit. The main artistic requirement was to refer, either symbolically or in the inscription, to Confederation or its anniversary. Any design changes would be on the reverses only, and the fifty-cent denomination was not included. An award of $500 was offered for each design accepted by the Finance Department.

This step towards a modernization of the coinage was doomed from the beginning by time limitations. Submissions had to be received by the middle of June, only one month after the contest began. The number of submissions was low, and their quality was not very high. No design was judged worthy of the $500 prize, let alone coining, for the ten-cent piece. In the remaining denominations, the winners were Gustav Hahn for the cent, and J.A.H. MacDonald for the five- and twenty-five cents. Unfortunately the winning designs were not announced until two months after the main celebrations on Dominion Day, and they never went further than the sketch stage.

Winning sketches
for the proposed Confederation
Commemorative coinage,
1927.
Public Archives Canada.

> *" Commemorative medals were the only part of the Diamond Jubilee project to be carried out by the Mint. "*

Commemorative medals were the only part of the Diamond Jubilee project to be carried out by the Mint. These medals were struck in very small numbers in gold, silver and tombac (a type of brass) for special presentation purposes. The obverse presents the uncrowned, conjoined busts of Queen Mary and King George. It was designed by English sculptor Percy Metcalfe, and the matrices and punches were prepared by the Royal Mint in London. The reverse depicts a crowned coat of arms within a maple wreath on which the motto A MARI USQUE AD MARE is inscribed below. This design was the work of Raymond Delamarre, and the master tools were made at the Paris Mint.

Bronze Confederation Commemorative medal, 1927.

The same designs were used for the smaller-size medal distributed to all school children that year, but the execution of the design was decidedly inferior. Over two million of these medals were issued.

During the long period of low demand there were signs that the Mint would resume the coining of gold. The Finance Department had finally ceased its purchasing of gold, and the Ontario Mining Association proposed to have sovereigns struck in return for gold deposits. In September 1925, the Mint cabled an urgent requisition to London for six pairs of sovereign dies. However it turned out that the coining of sovereigns was never to be resumed.

Canada raised the possibility that $5 and $10 gold coins might be produced once again by going back on the gold standard in 1926. The coat of arms used on the reverses of the gold coins of 1912 to 1914 was out of date since new armorial bearings had been assigned in 1921. Indeed it is doubtful whether the use of the shield portrayed on those coins had even been authorized! A new reverse design was needed in case the gold coinage should be revived. New master tools were ordered from the Royal Mint in London and were received in 1928. The demand for gold coinage never materialized, however, so we have only bronze trial strikes of the 1928 $5 and $10 to show us how the coins would have looked.

Bronze trial strikings for the proposed gold $5 and $10, 1928.

"The appointment went, however, to John H. Campbell..."

John Honeyford Campbell,
Deputy Master,
Ottawa Mint, 1925-1931,
Master, Royal Canadian Mint,
1931-1938.

In the summer of 1925, the relationship between the Canadian Government and the Royal Mint in London was further strained. Arthur Cleave, the Deputy Master of the Ottawa Mint, was in poor health. Despite lengthy absences from work, he clung to his post until August 1925. When Cleave's retirement was finally announced, Canadian officials let it be known through the High Commissioner in London that they would be pleased if H.E. Ewart, then Engineer in the Mechanics and Die Shop, might be appointed to fill the vacant post. Unlike Bonar and Cleave, Ewart was a Canadian and also related by blood to a member of the government. The appointment went, however, to John H. Campbell who had been Deputy Master of the Sydney Mint. Anglo-Canadian relations were worsened by the failure to consult the Finance Department prior to Campbell's appointment even though Canada had no legal right to expect such consultation. The Finance Department was particularly angry because Campbell was already sixty years old. Not only was he near retirement age, but his pension would have to be paid by Canada. (As time passed, the negative effects of Campbell's appointment were somewhat reversed by his obvious capability for the post. He also remained as Head of the Ottawa Mint much longer than he or anyone else expected, long after it was within the power of the government to replace him had they so wished.)

It is understandable that in such times of economic hardship there might be friction in the Royal Mint's branch plant system. There were some general as well as some quite specific problems.

In 1923, the London Royal Mint's Deputy Master made the first ever visit to the Ottawa Branch. This man, Col. Robert A. Johnson, justified the trip on the grounds that the possibility of internal changes and even cutbacks in Ottawa might require his personal presence. His visit became the subject of controversy (and remained so) for years. The Finance Department resented having to pay for Johnson's visit, especially since it was held by some that the trip was more in the nature of a vacation. Such questionable expenses were particularly disturbing to the Canadian Government at a time when its seigniorage revenues were so low.

In September of 1925, W.S. Fielding, by then in his late seventies, finally gave up the finance portfolio. His successor, James A. Robb, was to become known for his shrewd management, tax cutting and public debt reduction. In March 1926, he wrote to the Chancellor of the Exchequer, Winston Churchill. Reflecting the government's anger, he requested that the Canadian Government be provided with more detailed accounts of how the annual annuity for the Ottawa Mint was being spent. He also urged that Canada should be consulted in appointments. But the answer was unsympathetic: "The arrangements were identical with other Branch Mints, and there was no justification for the criticisms made."

In September 1927, Robb again approached Churchill through the High Commissioner. He focussed on the demand for some accounting of expenditures and worried particularly about the amounts designated as contingencies and retirement allowances. These tended to vary greatly and to prompt parliamentary questions. Churchill did not reply until April 1928. Although he had not changed his official position, he was willing to forgo legalities and give Robb the information he so dearly wanted. Churchill also raised the suggestion that the Minister might prefer to have the Mint transferred to Canadian control. Such a step could be easily accomplished, he said, if Canada forfeited the right to coin sovereigns.

Robb was not intrigued with this new prospect. He was only more determined than ever to have details of the expenses particularly from the years 1922 and 1923. Churchill apparently tried to prod Canada into assuming control of the Mint by deliberately giving Robb less than what he wanted. Churchill would only supply detailed expense accounts once a year for the previous calendar year.

The Canadian High Commissioner in London, P.C. Larkin, the tea magnate and financial benefactor of Prime Minister Mackenzie King, conveyed in no uncertain terms his view of this offer to Robb. He argued strongly for domestic ownership, contending that the government had been "entirely wrong" in not establishing its own mint instead of a branch back in 1901, and that Canada would never be satisfied "until our Mint is cut entirely adrift from the Government here."

However sympathetic Robb may have been to these sentiments, he stuck to his insistence upon receiving the accounts. In the summer of 1928, he carried his campaign into Whitehall by making a personal visit to Churchill. The desired accounting information was finally promised.

The restored profit-making in 1928 removed the urgency of the matter for the moment. The year finished as a very good one for the Mint. Earnings in excess of $300,000 amply covered

"... on December 1, 1931, ...the buildings, land and enterprise passed to Canadian hands."

the basic expenses. In November 1929, Finance Minister Robb died in office. The following year, the Liberals were swept from power in the general election. The new Prime Minister, R.B. Bennett, who also served initially as his own Finance Minister, visited Britain in November 1930. He discussed the Mint question personally with the Chancellor of the Exchequer, and came away resolved to take control for the country.

As Churchill had pointed out to Robb two years earlier, the procedure to be followed was not very difficult. Canada had only to pass an act giving up the right to coin sovereigns, and to make arrangements for the pensions of the British staff involved. With this done, the country would be free to establish its own mint on whatever terms seemed best. The necessary arrangements were quickly settled without any of the rancour that had characterized the dealings of the previous government and its High Commissioner with Whitehall.

In June of 1931, Prime Minister Bennett read the bill to establish the new Canadian Mint. By the end of the month, it was passed. The Liberals had established the Mint; now the Conservatives made it a wholly Canadian institution. The Discontinuance Proclamation went into effect on December 1, 1931, and the buildings, land and enterprise passed to Canadian hands.

The First Years of the Royal Canadian Mint

The mint which Canada took over was in many ways much more impressive than any of its original advocates, even the indomitable Senator McInnes, could have foreseen. Designed in an optimistic time, it was both physically and mechanically larger than McInnes had proposed. Its size and scope were, of course, one of the reasons it had finally been taken over: it had proven to be, as Courtney had worried back in 1901, inconveniently ample.

However cumbersome the facilities, they were under the control of the Finance Department. There was the possibility that after a decade of vulnerability, when new and embarrassing expenses seemed to occur regularly, the Mint might now be managed more parsimoniously.

The senior officers who had been appointed earlier by the Royal Mint, including J.H. Campbell, now styled the Master of the Royal Canadian Mint, continued in their positions. However appealing it might have been to replace them with Canadians from the country's vast pool of unemployed, their pension provisions made it impractical to permit any early retirements.

"... the predominant pressure on the Mint was not innovation but restraint."

Nor was this the only link with its parent institution which the Mint had not yet severed. Unable to produce its own matrices, the Mint still relied on England for these master tools which were needed to make the punches with which to sink dies. Because of the deepening depression, there was no possibility that the Mint would undertake the expense of outfitting itself to produce its own master tools.

Despite the brief surge in the demand for domestic coinage at the end of the 1920s, the predominant pressure on the Mint was not for innovation but restraint. It even seemed possible that far from issuing any new coins, the government might have to recall much of the surplus coinage issued a decade earlier. To date, there was no precedent for such redemption. In fact it was legally impossible to take back any coins unless they were "worn". Now with the economy in low gear, there was an estimated six million dollars in excess change in the country. The dishearteningly low requisitions for coins filed through the various Assistant Receivers General – a skimpy $665,000 in 1932 and only $480,000 in 1933 and $430,000 in 1934 – were questionable. In the face of the alleged surplus, these orders were best explained as local deficiencies. Thus, while most areas had vaults full of unwanted coins, a few needed more.

Even these false signs of economic health would diminish as the banks began to unload their surplus coins onto any branches needing them, in the face of the government's reluctance to redeem the excess. In the Mint's early idle days, coin production had been artificially stimulated by exporting U.S. silver. This time, practically all such coins had already been driven out of circulation by the weakness of the Canadian dollar. Not all functions of the Mint were as strongly curtailed as coinage.

Single Men's Association parading in Toronto, 1930s.
Public Archives Canada C-29397.

"Under such conditions the inadequacy of the old refining plant became apparent..."

It is a tempting but dangerous habit of commentators to put a label on a limited period of history. The misleading result is that any such period, however diverse in fact, tends to appear one-dimensional. So the Depression years are too often thought to have had no life or spirit at all. Even these years with all their poverty and unemployment and gloom saw stirring innovation and progress. Among the enterprises started at the time were the Canadian Broadcasting Corporation, the national airline which became Air Canada, and the Bank of Canada.

Likewise the mining industry continued its advance, making Canada a leader in mineral resources. The Royal Canadian Mint's connection to this industry through the Refinery Department helped to offset the slackness of its coining operations.

After the termination of shipments of South African Rand gold in 1918, the Refinery was again able to receive deposits of domestic gold. These deposits were considerably greater than Mint authorities expected, and continued to grow quickly. Staff who were underemployed in the Coining Department were kept busy in the Refinery. By 1931, total deposits had reached 1.8 million ounces.

Given such growth, it was not only impossible to do away with the temporary Refinery established in 1916, it had been essential to improve it during the 1920s.

Shortly before Canada assumed control of the Mint in 1931, the Finance Department took a number of steps to conserve the country's supply of gold, thereby altering the future of the refinery. Gold was being drawn to New York by the premium on the American dollar. In September, the Department adopted the practice of making up the difference to the producer by paying a premium on gold. The following month, licensing laws were imposed to prohibit the export of gold without Finance authority. The effect on the Refinery of these tactics was immediate; deposits doubled to 3.5 million ounces. The facilities had handled as much as a quarter of a million ounces a week during the Great War so this was not an impossible demand. But it did make anything resembling routine difficult. Overtime, once again, became commonplace.

Under such conditions, the inadequacy of the old refining plant became apparent, and requests for a major improvement of the facilities could no longer be ignored. In 1934, with the Refinery on its way to a record 3.8 million ounces, the government recognized the inevitable. Despite the grave state of the economy, authority was given for the creation of a new version of the Mint Refinery. For the first time, the problems of efficiency, supervision and loss of metal during processing would be properly addressed.

The new facility was located on a tri-
angular lot at the north side of the Mint.
A second storey walkway connected
the two buildings. It was designed as
a subsidiary of the Royal Canadian Mint
and, to harmonize with it, was constructed of Nepean sandstone in a Tudor
design. However the size and boldness
of the addition reflected the fact that
refining threatened to surpass in importance the principal undertaking
of the Mint.

New Refinery building,
1936.
Public Archives Canada PA-134851.

The new Refinery begun in March 1935 was operational by July 1936. Its success can be judged from the immediate increase in 1936 to over 4.5 million ounces of crude gold handled. Nor was its success short-lived. This sensible structure was designed in 1936 to meet any possible demand for many years to come. With twenty-four chlorination furnaces, the Refinery's capacity was about 600,000 ounces of fine gold trade bars per month, working normal hours.

Gold refining room, with chlorination furnaces at the left and tilting furnaces at the right, 1936. Public Archives Canada PA-132085.

" This sensible structure was designed in 1936 to meet any possible demand for many years to come."

1935

Emanuel Hahn

"...this could be accomplished equally well by producing a souvenir coin as by filling the needs for general circulation."

Within two months of the opening of the new Refinery, there were clear signs that the Canadian economy was finally beginning to recover. By early autumn, the Mint found that it was hard-pressed to satisfy the heavy demands for all denominations without working overtime. More than $1 million representing almost 17 million coins were issued that year. Although some of this was offset by the continuing withdrawal of worn coins, it represented a favourable and highly welcome sign. The recovery in the Mint's output of the late 1920s was of brief duration but this time the Mint would never again fall below the $1 million mark.

This return to volume in 1936 may have been encouraging, but the highlight of the coming years lay elsewhere. Prime Minister R.B. Bennett decided in October 1934 that Canada would finally issue a silver dollar. The year 1935, the silver jubilee of the reign of King George V and Queen Mary, would provide a splendid opportunity for the introduction of this new denomination. The government had economic as well as patriotic incentives for issuing the silver dollar. Not only would the silver mining industry receive a boost, but the government would gain by the move. The year 1934 was proving to be disastrous from the point of view of profit on coinage issue with the withdrawals of worn coins significantly exceeding new issues. Still the surplus of coins persisted. Earlier efforts to introduce a one-dollar coin had been defeated at least in part because it would not circulate. This now became a positive feature. The Mint's life depended on its continuing to produce coins. Obviously this could be accomplished equally well by producing a souvenir coin as by filling the needs for general circulation.

These justifications for the coin were sound. The immediate stimulus, however, came from a circular from the Royal Mint advertising its intention to issue a silver jubilee medal. It offered the Dominions the opportunity to participate in its production and sale. Literally within days of this overture, the Canadian Government announced in a cable to Britain its intention to issue a silver dollar for the silver jubilee.

Mint Master Campbell suggested that a new obverse portrait be obtained not only for the silver dollar but for all denominations of coins. He hoped this would pave the way for the eventual introduction of new reverse designs. Prime Minister Bennett proposed that the superimposed busts of King George and Queen Mary be featured on the obverse of the silver dollar. This idea was promptly squelched by the Deputy Master of the Royal Mint, Sir Robert A. Johnson. Such usage was unprecedented, except when a king and queen ruled jointly. The King's special consent would be required and, in any case, there was no time to work up new effigies so one of the existing heads would have to be used. Johnson, however, appeared sympathetic and eager to help. He recommended consideration of the King's portrait recently adopted for the silver coins of New Zealand, Southern Rhodesia and Mauritius.

Canada was not immediately interested in this suggestion. The Minister of Finance wanted to use the uncrowned portrait of the King in current use on the coins of Great Britain or, if that was impossible, to continue with the same effigy used on other Canadian coins together with the inscription GEORGIUS V REX ANNO REGNI XXV.

Once again Johnson rejected the Canadian ideas for the obverse. He said the King would likely reserve his uncrowned portrait for British use only. And he remained convinced that the new effigy by Percy Metcalfe was superior to the MacKennal bust in use in Canada. Finally he stressed that the reference to the King's title as Emperor of India must never be omitted. In order to avoid overcrowding of the obverse, he preferred to have the words ANNO REGNI XXV impressed on the edge of the coin, making way for the essential IND: IMP: or its equivalent.

Under the circumstances, Finance Minister Rhodes accepted the new effigy but declined to place part of the legend on the edge. The King's role as Emperor of India was referred to in the legend: GEORGIUS V REX *IMPERATOR* ANNO REGNI XXV. With the matter now all but settled, Johnson finally remarked upon the deletion of the customary DEI:GRA:, omission of which had stirred up such a furor in 1911. Johnson pointed out that this reference could be abbreviated to D:G:, but Rhodes stood by his decision to delete it altogether. Thus the 1935 silver dollar became Canada's only ''Godless'' coin of that denomination. Even the 1911 pattern dollar, unlike the issued domestic coins of that date, contained DEI: GRA: in the legend. Interestingly, there seems to have been no public objection to the legend on the 1935 dollar.

For the reverse design, Sir Robert Johnson suggested in view of the limited time available the coat of arms design approved for the $5 and $10 gold pieces in 1928 but never used for circulating coins. Canada had moved so swiftly, however, that Johnson's suggestion came too late.

Because time was short, the Government dispensed with a design competition and commissioned Emanuel Hahn, the renowned Toronto sculptor. He came to Ottawa in November 1934 with his design already sketched: a caribou. By this time, an informal advisory committee had been formed, consisting of Dr. Arthur Doughty, the Dominion Archivist; Eric Brown, Director of the National Gallery; B.J. Roberts of the Finance Department; Mint Master J.H. Campbell and E.J. Lemaire, Clerk of the Privy Council. They clearly liked Hahn's idea, but Finance Minister Rhodes wanted something different. The caribou had to wait until its use on the twenty-five cent piece a few years later.

Rhodes suggested a canoe with a voyageur or an Indian. Hahn worked the idea up into a drawing which pleased the Minister greatly. Within days Hahn was at work in his Toronto studio on the model. It was completed and on its way to London to be converted into a matrix by January 3, 1935. Despite the haste, the model proved satisfactory. Even Sir Robert Johnson was moved to compliment Canada on having produced such a fine coin. Prime Minister Bennett promptly released the previously secret details of the new coin nicknamed "the George".

Preliminary sketch
for silver dollar,
1935.
National Currency Collection, Ottawa.

"Canada had at last created a one-dollar coin."

Preliminary sketch
for silver dollar, 1935.

Silver dollar,
1935.

Silver dollar, 1936.

The proclamation giving the coin legal status went into effect on May 1, five days before the twenty-fifth anniversary of the King's accession. Canada had at last created a one-dollar coin.

The demand for the coin justified the government's hopes. The banks had gloomily predicted that only about 15,000 would be wanted, and did not even wish to handle the coin unless the government agreed to pay the shipping charges. Nearly half a million pieces were struck which gave needed work to the Mint. Special care and attention went into the production, consistent with the government's considerable profit on the issue. The coins were packed in cardboard tubes rather than shipped loose in canvas bags.

The silver dollar was intended to become a permanent feature of Canadian coinage. In 1936, some 336,900 were minted. The special commemorative obverse was not appropriate for this regular issue, and the master tools which were received for the abortive 1911 silver dollar were used to make the obverse dies. It was the first and last chance for the Mint to employ that obverse punch.

Modernization of Our Coinage Design

The Silver Jubilee celebrations, of which the new silver dollar was a part, ended suddenly when King George V died. Although he had been in deteriorating health in the autumn, he was sufficiently recovered to deliver his Christmas message to the Empire. However the King soon became gravely ill again and died just before midnight, January 20, 1936.

The Prince of Wales began his brief, stormy reign as King Edward VIII, and the Royal Mint began immediate preparations for his coinage effigies, both crowned and uncrowned, for the coins of Great Britain and the Empire.

This was the second time the Mint at Ottawa would receive matrices and punches bearing the portrait of a new sovereign. Unlike the previous occasion when delay had been foreseen early and yet had led to considerable inconvenience, this time it looked as if the transition would be smooth despite the increasing workload at the Mint.

Soon after the accession of the new King, Canada decided to take advantage of the event to introduce completely new coin designs. The leading advocate of this change was the Master of the Royal Canadian Mint, John H. Campbell, who had long sought to end what he termed "the sneering references to the numismatic art of the Dominion." It was Campbell who had initiated the design competition of 1927 and spearheaded ideas for a new five-cent design in 1930. Now in 1936, the intrepid old Mint Master finally won approval for radical change in the country's coinage designs.

_"...the change of monarch...
was a fitting opportunity
for innovation..."_

Although Canada was one of the first countries to make this decision, she was not alone. As Campbell stressed in his arguments, the change of monarch, despite Royal Mint assertions that it seldom left time for new designs, was a fitting opportunity for innovation. Several other countries including New Zealand, Australia, South Africa and finally Britain herself went through a design revision process.

King Edward VIII,
December 1936.
Public Archives Canada C-5144.

Once again, Canada requested permission to use on its obverses an uncrowned effigy more in keeping with its increasingly independent status. This time Canada together with the other three Dominions received permission to employ the new uncrowned portrait of King Edward VIII. It had been designed by the renowned Thomas Humphrey Paget for the British coinage, and was approved for Canadian use by mid-August following an elaborate selection process.

" ...King Edward... considered his left to be his "best side"."

The new effigy faced left, as had the effigy of King George V, thereby breaking the tradition started with King Charles II to portray each new monarch facing in the direction opposite to his predecessor. This was done at the insistence of King Edward, who considered his left to be his "best side".

Plaster model
for Edward VIII Canadian coinage obverses.
National Currency Collection,
Ottawa.

"... The government gave up its insistence upon Canadian artists..."

The Canadian Government was now confronted with the challenge of finding five suitable reverse designs. While the new one- and five-cent coins of 1920 and 1922 were innovative in their time, they provided no basis for a series. A possible theme was suggested by the much-admired coins introduced by Ireland in 1928. Sometimes termed the "barnyard" series, they demonstrated what could be achieved by the depiction of indigenous animal species. New Zealand had recently issued coins with a somewhat similar concept. Canada had ample animal subjects for consideration.

But the design selection committee, hoping that the submitting artists would suggest something so far overlooked, left its guidelines quite general. Themes such as mining, fishing, transportation and flora were also suggested, but the committee made it clear that contestants were left free to choose any other subjects which might appeal to them individually. Invitations were sent in April 1936 to twelve Canadian artists.

Of the seventy-six drawings submitted, six were selected by the design committee for the consideration of Prime Minister King and Finance Minister Dunning. They promptly rejected them all. Beautiful drawings of a polar bear and a Canada goose were considered unsuitable because they seemed to confirm Canada's image as an Arctic wilderness. Thus, after months of searching, little had been accomplished and the need for a decision was becoming more urgent.

The Government gave up its insistence upon Canadian artists and, as so often before, appealed for help from the Royal Mint. The Prime Minister, who took a keen interest in the matter, had already decided that one denomination should symbolize Canada. Sir Robert Johnson, still Deputy Master of the Royal Mint, cabled Lord Tweedsmuir, the Governor General of Canada, for some ideas. Tweedsmuir responded with suggestions for a series of animal subjects and a series on an historical theme with designs comparable to that already in use on the silver dollar. Johnson invited the well-known artists, George E. Kruger-Gray and Percy Metcalfe, to work on the project and, as an afterthought, added Frank Dobson. The Canadian Government objected to paying all three artists so Dobson's fee was not charged to Canada's account. Prime Minister King felt that Kruger-Gray and Metcalfe, together with the Canadian artists who were still working on designs, would provide sufficient material for selection.

By July, the Government had decided that the Canadian Coat of Arms should adorn the fifty-cent coin, and was beginning to express some more definite ideas about the other denominations. A maple twig was being contemplated for the cent, a caribou for the five cents, a mountain goat or a mountain peak for the ten cents and a fishing schooner for the twenty-five cents. There was no thought of replacing Hahn's voyageur design on the silver dollar. By the end of the month, Johnson was able to send to Canada photographs of the designs prepared in Britain.

Preliminary sketch
for the 50 cents,
1937.

Sketch for the "caribou" 25 cents,
1937.

Preliminary sketches
for "caribou" 5 cents,
1937.

Plaster model
for "schooner"
25 cents,
1937.

In September, Finance Department officials in consultation with wildlife experts had made their selections from all the British and Canadian drawings and proposed various revisions. Kruger-Gray's Canadian Coat of Arms with supporting figures was selected for the fifty cents with a recommendation for changing the lettering. Hahn's caribou design was chosen for the twenty-five cent rather than the five cents. Originally it had the Big Dipper constellation in the background, but this was later removed. The fishing schooner, also by Hahn and modelled primarily if not exclusively after the famous Nova Scotian ship, *Bluenose*, was the choice for the ten cents. The denomination was originally in two lines and it was suggested that "10 CENTS" should be placed on one line.

The *Bluenose*
under full sail.
Public Archives Canada
PA-30803.

"It was decided to continue minting 1936-dated coins..."

Preliminary sketch for "beaver" 10 cents, 1937.

A beaver design submitted by Kruger-Gray for the ten cents was designated for the five cents instead. However the beaver had to be redrawn to make its appearance more realistic, and revised lettering was required. Two maple leaves on a sprig, Kruger-Gray's conception for the five cent, was chosen with slight modifications for the cent.

Preliminary sketch for cent. 1937.

The two successful artists were in a position to begin work on their models by late September. Hahn's work could not be completed before Christmas, which meant the dies for the ten- and twenty-five-cent pieces would not be ready before March 1937. Yet it seemed likely that Canada would have at least the new one- and five-cent dies to begin the year.

Despite heavy coinage demands on the Royal Mint, most of the master tools required for the various 1937 coinages for both Britain and the colonies were ready by late 1936. In all tools for more than two hundred dies had been prepared.

In December 1936, King Edward VIII announced his abdication. All of the artwork and technology that had gone into preparing the obverse dies throughout the year had been in vain. The Royal Mint would have to begin all over again with new sittings for portraits, new models from the portraits and new die-making tools from the models. The obverse dies portraying Edward's younger brother, King George VI, were desperately needed for the beginning of the year but could not possibly be available for months.

As in 1910, Canada had taken the precaution of stockpiling extra coins for the transitional period. Still the possibility existed that supplies might be exhausted. It was decided to continue minting 1936-dated coins using the obsolete King George V dies with the old reverses. Thus in the first quarter of 1937, some 678,823 one cents, 191,237 ten cents and 153,322 twenty-five cents of this type were produced. At least some of the reverse dies for this extraordinary posthumous coinage were marked with a small dot.[1]

King George VI,
1937.
Public Archives Canada
PA-52563.

Plaster model
for George V Canadian
coinage obverses.

New Canadian coinage, 1937.

However the anticipated shortage did not materialize. This was attributable to the volume of coins on hand, the relatively low demand at the time, and especially the grace with which the new King obliged the Royal Mint's artists with special sittings. (A new effigy was already completed and approved by February 11). Most of the "1936 dot" coins were not needed. Only the twenty-five-cent piece was actually issued. A few rare examples of the cent and ten cents do survive,[2] all of the others apparently having been melted down.

Because of the extraordinary pressure on the Royal Mint caused by the abdication, all obverse and reverse models for the Canadian coins were delivered to the Paris Mint for reduction into matrices and punches. The precedent had already been set when Paris produced die-making tools for one of the 1927 medals commemorating the Diamond Jubilee of Confederation. The work of the Paris Mint was equal in quality to that of London, and the tools were finished there in good time. The dies for the four smaller denominations were received by the Canadian Mint in time to issue the new coins on May 14, just two days after the Coronation.

The Paris Mint had problems with the fifty-cent dies, and the dollar obverse was delayed through a misunderstanding, so these denominations were held up for several months. In any case, the Royal Canadian Mint had never attached much importance to the simultaneous release of all the new coins.

When the production began in Ottawa, there were still some technical difficulties. Only the cent was free of problems. On the five cents, the King's eyebrow appeared flat and defective because of the amount of metal needed to strike up a coin in such high relief. Likewise on the ten cents, the amount of metal demanded by the obverse on such a small coin did not leave enough to bring up the sails and rigging properly on the reverse. The twenty-five cents presented similar problems. The King's jaw and ear on the obverse, and the brow of the caribou on the reverse were not being struck clearly.

The Paris Mint had produced trial pieces for all denominations except the dollar on thick brass planchets, and thus had experienced no problems with the five and twenty-five cents. The trial pieces had been produced with upset[3] reverses unlike Canadian coins which had been struck since 1908 with the straight[3] reverses. Sir Robert Johnson suggested that Canada might do well to employ upset reverses, but this advice was ignored. Instead the problems were eventually resolved by making slight technical modifications which did not affect the designs.

Johnson had remarked that the difficulties with the ten- and twenty-five-cent coins showed that Hahn, unlike Kruger-Gray, did not understand the fundamentals of modelling coinage reverses. We have no record of how, or whether, Johnson explained himself when the fifty-cent denomination, modelled by Kruger-Gray, presented the most serious and persistent difficulties of all. The obverse consumed so much metal that the shield on the reverse struck up very poorly. But such problems, however troublesome to the Mint staff, were little noticed by the general public. The coins were received with wide acclaim.

For the first time since 1912, the Mint produced cased sets of specimen coins for sale in quantity to the public. Sets of the six coins with a satin or "matte" finish, packaged in cardboard boxes, were sold through the Bank of Canada. Nearly 1,300 such sets were produced and sold in 1937-38. The quality of these coins was definitely inferior to the specimen coins regularly produced by the Mint. Indeed much finer pieces with mirror fields and frosted devices and lettering were struck in smaller numbers for private distribution in leather-covered cases to dignitaries and others.

1936 "dot" silver 10 cents, struck in 1937.

Contemporaneous with the construction of a new refinery, the introduction of a silver dollar and the development of the new reverse designs, the Royal Canadian Mint moved towards foreign coin work which could provide activity and income during otherwise slack periods. Early in 1936, the West Indian island of the Dominican Republic inquired whether Canada could strike its coins.

Unlike the small non-Canadian coinages done almost twenty years earlier, the amount in question here was far from negligible. Newfoundland and Jamaica had required only 2.5 million pieces over a three-year period, but the Dominican Republic was now seeking more than five million immediately. There was more than profit and activity involved in the proposal. This contract would represent the first work done for a country outside the British Empire. The Dominican coinage had formerly been provided by the mints in Philadelphia, Berlin and London, and its production in Ottawa could enhance the Mint's prestige.

One difficulty was that the Dominican Republic was not regarded as a reliable country to do business with. It had been racked by economic and political problems throughout its history culminating in bankruptcy in 1905. The United States Marines had just left after eighteen years of occupation, and there were some signs of recovery under the new President, Trujillo Molina. He backed material progress, but his tactics were considered dictatorial.

Canada might justifiably ignore the Dominican Republic's politics but the proposal still had to be closely examined from the financial angle. The contract might not have been signed, but the Royal Bank of Canada had a branch in the Republic and was willing to accept financial responsibility and to act as agent for its government. That settled, legislation was passed in Canada granting the Finance Department power to enter into coinage contracts with foreign countries, subject to authorization by the Governor General. However no contract would be allowed to interfere with the production of coinage for domestic needs as the contract with Jamaica had threatened to do in 1919.

While this lengthy legal process was taking place, designers had been working on models based on sketches done in the Dominican Republic for its first coinage of the twentieth century. The Mint was still unable to produce the master tools, and once more referred this aspect of the work to the Royal Mint in London.

Five denominations were involved: the bronze one centavo, cupro-nickel five centavos and silver ten centavos, twenty centavos and half peso. Although all had the same reverse design, the country's coat of arms, two obverses were involved. The design for the one centavo was a palm tree similar to that of the 1923 British West African coinage. For the remaining denominations, a figure of Liberty was prepared by T.H. Paget, designer of the new King George VI obverses.

Dominican Republic coinage, 1937.

" The coins were received with wide acclaim."

The punches and matrices arrived from Britain in November 1937. Despite near-record production of Canadian coinage, the whole Dominican order had been struck and shipped by the end of March 1938 further enhancing the reputation of the Royal Canadian Mint.

The public interest in commemorative coins was growing in the 1930s. Such coins had been struck by the United States for decades, but they had not appeared in the British Empire in recent years until Australia issued a commemorative florin in 1927. It marked the establishment of Canberra as the country's capital. Canada did not enter the field until 1935, but with the Australian precedent, there was growing expectation of a commemorative coin for any suitable occasion.

The Canadian Government, however, declined to issue a coin for the Coronation of King George VI despite calls both in the streets and in Parliament for such an observance. Perhaps to compensate for this omission, it supported proposals for a Royal Visit commemorative when it was announced late in 1938 that the following summer the King would become the first reigning sovereign to visit his Canadian domain.

The historic credentials of the event were indisputable, and besides, there was the likelihood of a large profit. Silver was worth only 43 cents per ounce, and only .6 ounces were needed to produce a silver dollar. But there was a lack of enthusiasm from, all places, the Royal Canadian Mint. J.H. Campbell, now in his early seventies, had just retired. His successor was H.E. Ewart who had been the Finance Department's candidate for the position in 1925.

Ewart was worried that the government did not seem to be allowing sufficient time to handle the task professionally. He anticipated, with good reason, that the demand for any commemorative coins would be unprecedented. Thus more time had to be allowed for production, apart from the several months it might take for the Royal Mint to produce matrices and punches. The Mint could not produce more than half a million silver dollars in three months. Yet there was the possibility of over one million being needed, more than the total of all silver dollars produced to date.

The government favoured a new obverse featuring both the King and the Queen (which would require lengthy sittings in Britain if it were allowed at all), as well as a complicated reverse suggesting the significance of their visit. Ewart preferred the much less ambitious scheme of using the existing dual Coronation portrait on the twenty-five-cent piece.

The government prevailed in its desire to issue a commemorative silver dollar, but at least the Mint's warning was heeded. By the middle of November, the idea of a time-consuming special obverse was abandoned. For the reverse design, the new War Memorial scheduled to be unveiled by the King in Ottawa's Victory Square received strong consideration. The government settled instead upon the attractive simplicity of the Parliament Buildings particularly the Peace Tower. There was still some question concerning the best format. To emphasize the Royal Tour, it was thought to depict both King and Queen standing crowned before the buildings. But this design would have taken too long to produce. Some cabinet ministers then suggested the personal monograms of the King and Queen on opposite sides of the Tower. Finally the Peace Tower and Centre Block were left to stand alone.

Clarity and simplicity were also important in choosing the inscription to surround the image. Originally conceived as the lengthy "Happy is he who reigns in the hearts of his people", it was replaced by "He reigns by the faith of his people" rendered in Latin as "FIDES SVORVM REGNAT. Prime Minister Mackenzie King suggested the final touch: the insertion of the figure "1" making this the only dollar with a numerical designation.

Original sketch
for Royal Visit silver dollar,
1939.
National Currency Collection.

Royal Visit silver dollar,
1939.

As in the case of the 1935 dollar, Canada did not seek outside help in the preparation of either the design or the plaster model of the coin. This work was contracted directly to Emanuel Hahn of Toronto. He accomplished most of the design work in only four weeks.

To aid in production, a large new coining press was purchased. It could strike up to 100 pieces a minute at a maximum pressure of 250 tons. By the middle of December, the Prime Minister was able to issue a press release. He noted that "a great deal of time and consideration had been given to the choice of a suitable design." Canada had demonstrated its ability to produce an impressive design and to do so quickly.

One serious problem remained. Traditionally, artists were permitted to initial their work. However inconspicuous on the coin, the tiny letters were a source of pride to the designer. But suddenly, the Cabinet took the firm stand that this design could only be accepted with no initials. Hahn's original model presented an oversized version of his initials positioned on either side of the Peace Tower — an unhappy choice since Cabinet had considered displaying the King's and Queen's initials in a similar way.

Hahn was prepared to alter both the size and position of his initials, but stated that as an artist he "could not entirely accept the government decision." However the government refused to consider any alternatives and proceeded without Hahn's approval. In fact the Prime Minister was prepared to issue a statement that Hahn had no reason to complain, since initials had been allowed in the past only through oversight. Ewart managed to persuade the government not to make such a ludicrous statement, but was unable to change the decision to omit the initials. Hahn had to be satisfied with a veiled apology from Ewart to the effect that the decision had been taken at a level over his head.

There were delays in forwarding the model to Britain, but the dies were ready in time for the Mint. After several weeks of overtime, adequate supplies of the coin were on hand before the Royal Family arrived. The King was presented with specimens, and Hahn, even if not identified on the coins themselves, was publicly acknowledged as the designer.

Nearly 1.4 million of the silver dollars were prepared for distribution through not only the usual banking channels, but the Post Office as well. A small proportion of the coins remained unsold, and just over 150,000 of them were melted down between 1939 and 1945.

The government also decided upon
an issue of medals to celebrate
the Royal Visit. Although the Mint had
acquired an engraving machine to foster
the growth of its Medal Department,
these facilities had seldom been
employed in the past decade. Apart
from striking interesting medals
for the International Mathematical Congress in 1936 and the Webster Memorial Medal for Good Airmanship in 1938,
most of the work of the Medal Department had been in the preparation
of plates for printing the signatures
on the Bank of Canada note issues.

Now there was an opportunity to display
the Mint's capabilities for medal production. Three series of commemorative
medals were made: one for presentation to the Royal Family and other dignitaries; one for distribution to school
children; and a third for sale to the public. The design was to be the same on all
three series: only the size and material
would differ.

A group met with Emanuel Hahn in November 1938 to discuss the commemorative dollar and the medal design. They
relayed to him the Prime Minister's
notion of highlighting the Royal Tour's
itinerary on a map of Canada. Above
the map, Hahn added Canada's Coat
of Arms with its familiar motto, 'A MARI
USQUE AD MARE,' and below, the inscription 'REGEM ET REGINAM CANADA
SALVTAT' — "Canada salutes her King
and Queen."

From the very first, the obverse sought
was the dual effigy used on Britain's
1937 Coronation medal and so
frequently requested by Canada
for coinage use. The British gave
permission to use this obverse
in December. The government had
already approved Hahn's sketch
for the reverse. It appeared
that the medal might be completed
as quickly as the 1939 silver dollar
had been.

Then just before Christmas, doubts
arose whether any medals would be
produced at all. Mint Master Ewart
was well aware of the expense involved
and of the great stress the undertaking
would put on the Mint. Earlier he had
sought to restrict production to the small
quantity required for presentation purposes. Now he suggested that the new
map reverse be placed on the fifty-cent
piece. Canada would have its third commemorative coin and the Mint a tidy
profit rather than the expense of creating
large numbers of medals to be given
away.

The government rejected any changes.
It insisted on the use of the double
portrait which could not be used on
a coin to provide some recognition
of the Queen's part in the tour. The design question was finally settled in late
January.

Now further delays occurred. Hahn fell behind schedule in producing the model from which the master tools were to be prepared. Ewart commented, "It seems impossible to impress upon him that time is just as important as a few stray islands around Baffin Land." Meanwhile in London, the Royal Mint's artist, Percy Metcalfe, had to make changes to the obverse model. The lateness of both models caused conflicts in the Royal Mint's scheduling. It would be another three months before even two of the required three sets of master tools were completed.

As in 1927, Canada was in danger of being forced to issue a medal to commemorate an event long after its passage. And as in 1927, the London Mint solved the problem by resorting to outside help. Given the need for over 2.5 million pieces, the school children's medal had to enter production first. It did not have to meet the rigid standards of the other medals so production of the dies was contracted out to a Winnipeg firm. The task of engraving the master tools was entrusted to the firm's finest engraver, Thomas Shingles. Later in the year, he would join the staff of the Royal Canadian Mint and serve as its Chief Engraver for many years. Production began with the dies engraved by Shingles. When the Metcalfe obverse arrived from England, however, it was employed for all subsequent strikings.[4]

Royal Visit presentation
medal, tombac, 1939

At first it was feared that production
of the master tools for the larger medals
would have to be contracted out as well,
but the Royal Mint was able to complete
and deliver them on time. The Royal
Canadian Mint with much overtime
managed to meet the challenge of striking the medals.

The 1¼ inches medals in silver and
bronze for the general public were marketed through the country's twelve thousand post offices. Sales of the silver
medals exceeded 58,000 pieces, sold at
50 cents each, and over 216,000 bronze
medals were sold at 10 cents each.
These medals were larger in diameter
than the bronze medals given out
to the school children.

Gold specimens of the special 3 inches
presentation medals were received
by the King and Queen while Prin-
cesses Elizabeth and Margaret Rose
were given medals in silver. The medals
for the Royal Family were personally
presented on May 20 by the Finance
Minister at the Parliamentary Dinner
three days after the tour began.

Various dignitaries received silver or
tombac[5] presentation medals. Prime
Minister Mackenzie King received a set
of three, in gold, silver and tombac,
while a gold medal was given
to President Roosevelt.

Under great strain, the Royal Canadian
Mint managed to complete its largest
issue of commemorative medals on time
while meeting a steady demand for coinage. This was only achieved by working
three eight-hour shifts when necessary.
But even this was relative idleness
compared to the hyperactivity which was
about to begin.

13

Notes:

[1] On the cent, the dot is just below the date; on the ten and twenty-five cents, it is below the ribbon tying the wreath at the bottom. Only the above three denominations have been found with a dot.

[2] Of the few surviving pieces, only one, a cent, is a circulation strike; the remainder are specimen strikes not intended for issue as currency.

[3] Normally coins are struck with either of two obverse-reverse orientations. When a coin is held vertically with obverse design right side up and is turned on its vertical axis, the reverse will appear right side up with the "straight reverse" or "medal" arrangement, or it will appear upside down with the "upset reverse" or "coinage" arrangement.

[4] Metcalfe's obverse is clearly superior to Shingles' effort. The two can be distinguished by observing the bottom of the bust which runs right down to the edge on the Shingles obverse.

[5] Tombac is a kind of brass consisting of 88 percent copper and 12 percent zinc.

Coinage During the War Years

Barely two months after the Royal Tour was over and King George and Queen Elizabeth had returned to Britain with their mementos, war broke out in Europe. In retrospect, Canada's newly erected War Memorial might indeed have been more suitable than the serene Peace Tower as a reverse for the commemorative dollar and as a sign of the times. On September 1, 1939, Hitler invaded Poland. Soon the great fear of the previous decade became fact: Canada was at war.

In contrast with the events of 1914, when the effect of the war did not reach the economy until several years after the fighting started, the reaction this time was immediate. To help supply Britain and her allies, Canadian agriculture and industry increased their output.

The Mint too felt the impact of the events abroad. Within a month of Canada's declaration of war, orders for coinage from the Mint already exceeded its normal production capability and could only be met by working overtime. In a mere twelve weeks, over 27 million pieces were struck. Even though this demand did not start until autumn, the value of coins issued that year was more than double that of 1938.

" ... the Mint's output jumped dramatically to more than 128 million pieces ... "

While Mint officials were at first pleased at the rise in demand after nearly two decades of calm, the increases were alarming. It was perhaps only the belief that this war, unlike the Great War, could not last very long that made the accompanying stress tolerable. Troops had been drawn up along the Maginot Line — Britain and France on one side, Germany on the other — but there was little real combat. Confidence in an early peace was widespread.

Despite this expectation, the domestic economic expansion continued. Throughout the first half of 1940, the demands on the Mint reflected the activity of the country. Fourteen-hour days were required as early as February, a month when production was usually very low. These tiring schedules continued throughout the spring.

Between April and June 1940, the Germans invaded Denmark, Holland, Belgium and, ultimately, France. The "phoney war" was over. With it went the prospect of peace in the immediate future. The already strained industrial facilities of the nation increased their efforts another degree.

This resulted in such an increase in the demand for coinage that the Mint expanded to two and, in some departments, three shifts. Over fifty new men joined the staff. These were mainly apprentices who required a high level of supervision. In addition, the administration had to deal with the extra security checks which the new shifts entailed.

Although many men were employed, the final obstacle to coping with soaring demand was the machinery. The bottleneck was at the rolling mills. The seven coining presses were capable of a total of five million coins per week, but the mills could yield only half as many blanks. This problem was solved by purchasing bronze blanks for the cents from a private firm. This released for other tasks men both from the melting room which prepared the metal for the rolling mills, and from the cutting room which punched the blanks from the rolled metal.

As a consequence, the Mint's output jumped dramatically to more than 128 million pieces, three times the record set the previous year, and more than four times the Mint's regular capacity. This included 600,000 coins in one-, five- and ten-cent denominations, struck for the Government of Newfoundland. The island's coinage requirement had been minimal for the past twenty years, but an influx of Canadian servicemen created a sudden need for small change.

The Royal Mint was too busy with its own urgent work to undertake the Newfoundland coinage within a reasonable time. In October, the Royal Canadian Mint was asked to do the work. Sets of punches, sent on loan to Ottawa, arrived in mid-November. Since it was expected that Canada would supply all of Newfoundland's coinage requirements until the end of the war, the punches were left undated. Thus the small number of required dies could be completed by hand allowing dates to be changed without raising new punches every year. Despite the nuisance of having to prepare silver alloy of a higher standard of fineness than that adopted twenty years before by Canada, the last of the Newfoundland order was shipped only one month after receipt of the punches.

In the view of Mint Master Ewart, the Mint's great exertion of 1940 had set a record which must stand "for many years to come." As it happened, it stood for only three years. In 1943, after another two years of overtime and double and triple shifts, the 1940 record was surpassed by a new total of 153 million pieces achieved at the rate of three million per week, (a total which not long before had been the output for a whole year).

The need for overtime and extra shifts continued well into 1945 by which time more than 650 million pieces had been produced. Only then did the demand for coinage begin to ease slightly. In the midst of this heavy demand, the Mint managed to make time to prepare coinage for Newfoundland. After completion of its coinage for 1944, Newfoundland finally reduced its silver alloy from 925 fine to 800 fine, the Canadian standard.

This impressive wartime output by the Mint was achieved with facilities only slightly improved since the Mint opened. Certainly the number of staff and the number of man-hours were increased significantly, and prepared bronze blanks were purchased outside the Mint beginning in 1940. Yet, basically, it was the Mint which had existed before the war that produced the record coinage of wartime.

Some improvements were made after 1939. An additional rolling press was purchased. There was also the acquisition of high-frequency electric melting furnaces to handle the silver and bronze alloys more quickly; a planchet rimming machine; and a centrifugal machine for drying coins and blanks. But generally, it was not improved technology which permitted the increased output, but rather manpower, and in some respects, human ingenuity.

Pouring coinage bars,
1940s.
Public Archives Canada
PA-134856.

Passing coinage bars
through powerful rolling
mills to make strip,
1940s.
Public Archives Canada
PA-132090.

Passing strip through a
blanking press,
1940s.
Public Archives Canada
PA-132086.

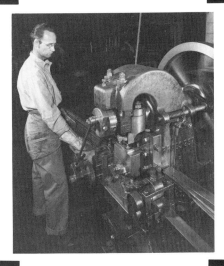

"It was not until 1945 that all dies were chromium-plated."

One innovation concerned the coinage dies. Increased coin production put pressure on the die-making facilities. Die consumption for the year 1938 was about 1,000, rising to nearly 4,000 in 1943. The impossibility of using unskilled labour in die production made it essential to discover some means of extending die life, and thereby keeping the requirements as low as possible.

In general, the greater the diameter of the coin, the shorter the average die life. Prior to 1943, a single pair of silver dollar dies had struck a maximum of 45,000 pieces whereas a pair of one-cent dies had been known to strike 700,000 pieces. This discrepancy was unavoidable; the object was to achieve the maximum for each denomination. The key to extended die life was found to be the steel itself and the attention given to its preparation. Other factors such as the quality of the die cut, the condition of the blanks and the talent of the press operator were all studied and improved. But the most important factor was to begin with high standard steel. This was particularly difficult during the war years when all metals were in short supply. But even a slight improvement in steel quality was reflected in prolonged die life.

It was to counteract just this problem of poor metal that the Mint began in 1942 to chromium-plate the faces of some one- and five-cent dies. Chromium-plating had been used on the five-cent coin press collars as early as 1930 to protect them from damage by the rough edges of the nickel blanks. The process gave improved durability on signature plates for the Finance Department as well. Now it was found not only to extend the life of the coinage dies, but also to impart an attractive mirror-like finish to the coins (rather than the previous frosted appearance).

Because the process was laborious, only one die face at a time was plated. Thus some coins produced between 1942 and 1944 feature the glossy finish on one side and the old frosted finish on the other. It was not until 1945 that all dies were chromium-plated. Nevertheless, chromium-plating was an important factor which, by 1945, allowed each die pair to yield as many as five million pieces.

The heavy demands on the Mint's capacity during the war put an abrupt end to silver dollar production. The war years brought other changes mainly imposed by metal shortages and by the volume of coinage involved. The one- and five-cent pieces caused problems because both copper and nickel were in short supply. Although the one-cent piece was subject to the most attention, it underwent no visible change.

The Americans also wanted to reduce copper consumption, and the War Consumption Board in Washington experimented with a variety of alternative materials. At one point, even plastic was considered, but the Americans eventually settled on zinc-plated steel cents. The Royal Canadian Mint rejected this solution because Ewart feared production difficulties could result from zinc becoming lodged in the dies. He also pointed out that the one- and ten-cent pieces might be confused if they were suddenly issued in the same colour. However, the Stanley Steel Co. of Hamilton did experiment with copper-plated steel for cent blanks, and a few trial pieces were struck by the Mint.

The Canadian Bankers' Association suggested a three-cent coin. It would save copper and, presumably, production time and it would be useful since many items of the day such as newspapers and stamps, cost three cents. The suggested format was a triangle with rounded points, or a round coin with a hole in the centre to differentiate it from existing coins. The Mint examined the idea but dropped it when it appeared the design and production time would outweigh any benefit.

In the end, the only change made involving the cent was a slight alteration in its composition. This alteration stemmed from a shortage not of copper but of tin, the amount of which was reduced from three percent to one-half percent. In March 1942, it was proposed to eliminate tin from the bronze alloy altogether, but this would have required an Act of Parliament. Instead a trace of tin was retained to comply with existing regulations. Since the exact composition of coinage bronze was not legislated, the change was made without the public being notified.

"A more radical change was reserved for the five-cent piece."

A more radical change was reserved for the five-cent piece. Nickel was scarce. The United States required all its own output and much of Canada's for munitions. Canada could no longer obtain its five-cent blanks from American companies even though the nickel originally came from Canadian mines. This problem had long been foreseen by the Mint, and various replacements for nickel were now considered. These included an alloy containing a low amount of silver which the United States had adopted for their five-cent piece in 1942. It was ruled out because of its cost and its tendency to acquire a distracting pink discolouration in circulation. Cupro-nickel was rejected because adequate supplies could not be assured. Ewart, therefore, advised the Finance Department that his preference was for tombac. To overcome possible confusion with the cent, he recommended that the five-cent piece be made twelve-sided (dodecagonal) inspired by the brass threepence introduced by Great Britain in 1937.

Ewart also passed on a suggestion by Robert Edmunds, the Chief of the Coining and Medal Division. He had proposed that a small "V" be added under each of the maple leaves on the existing reverse design to remind the public that the change was part of the war effort. He thought this might "assist in overcoming the psychological reaction that often occurs when excited folks fear the currency is being tampered with". A decision on the small "Vs" was postponed pending advice from the Department of Justice about the proper legal procedure for the introduction of a new design. The response was so long · in coming that when approval was given, the five-cent coin stocks were too low to allow consideration of a new design.

Proposed designs
for the "Victory" five-cent piece,
1942.

Robert J. Edmunds,
Chief of the Coining and Medal Division,
1939-1955.

Nickel round five cents,
1942.

Tombac 12-sided five cents,
1942.

Thus the tombac coins were issued
in the late summer of 1942 without any
design change apart from the new
twelve-sided shape and the omission
of the denticles around the rim on both
obverse and reverse sides. The coins
were hoarded by the public partly as
a curiosity and partly because of a widespread suspicion that they would be
withdrawn soon after issue, and thus
become valuable rarities.

Meanwhile work continued on new
designs for the tombac coin. Several
designs were created, all featuring as
their central device Churchill's famous
"V for Victory." The selected design
was a single large "V" in conjunction
with a torch, and a brief message
in International Code. The Finance
Department altered the coded message to a longer phrase to be inscribed
on the perimeter of the reverse: "We
win when we work willingly." The artist
was Thomas Shingles, who had been
employed by the Mint since 1939 and
became the chief engraver in 1943.
He cut the matrix for the reverse,
the first coinage master tool made
entirely in Canada. The work was done
entirely by hand since the Mint did
not possess a reducing machine at that
time. The historic matrix has been
preserved, and is now on loan from
the Mint to the National Currency Collection in the Bank of Canada, Ottawa.

Some of the proposed
designs for the "Victory"
five-cent piece,
1943.

Tombac five cents,
1943.

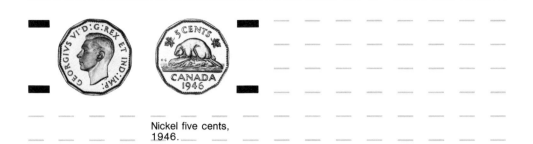

Nickel five cents,
1946.

But the evolution of the "nickel" was not yet complete. In a sudden reversal of its earlier recommendations, the Mint withdrew its support for the tombac composition. The extra work involved in preparing tombac blanks in place of the ready-made blanks previously used was more than the overworked Mint could undertake. A chromium-plated steel five-cent piece continuing with the new reverse was agreed upon, and first issued in 1944.

Much thought was given to an explanation for this, the third alteration of the five-cent piece since 1942. Neither the Finance Department nor the Mint could accept the other's version of the truth. The former was ready to say that the change was needed because the Mint could not handle the current demands. The Mint found this unfair considering its accomplishments. The Mint proposed a blunt statement that the change was made because the public disliked the tombac coins. This was thought to reflect badly on the Finance Department which bore ultimate responsibility for the choice of metal. As a compromise, the public was told that the change depended on a shortage of both components of tombac, namely copper and zinc.

Whatever the explanation, the new steel coins were sufficiently popular with all parties to survive until the use of nickel was resumed after the war. In fact by early 1945, supplies of nickel were sufficient to permit this metal's use in coinage, but the government continued to issue the steel coins throughout the year. This was done as a gesture to the Stanley Steel Co. which had gone to some trouble and expense in order to supply the steel blanks. The standard nickel coins with their familiar beaver design were reintroduced in 1946. They retained the twelve-sided shape, and the tombac coins began to be withdrawn.

14

The Business of Medals

Military medals were one of the countless needs created by the war in Europe. Although it was extremely busy, the Royal Canadian Mint was the logical place to manufacture them.

There had been a lull in activity in the production of medals after the creation of the Royal Visit commemoratives. This was to be expected, and in view of the increased coinage volume of the Mint, it was welcomed. But the Mint's concern with medals had not ceased. It was now providing medals for the Royal Canadian Mounted Police as well as the Engineering Institute and the Royal Society of Canada.

In addition to its annual medal work, the Mint produced an unusual piece for the Department of External Affairs in 1944. It served as an award for students in the Republic of Brazil who excelled in the study of Canadian history and geography. This new and complex medal was not only engraved by hand, like the Royal Society medals, but was also designed by Shingles. Twenty-five were struck.

Thus the involvement in medals had enjoyed a slow but steady growth. It was to provide a sound basis for the production of war medals soon to be in demand.

" ... a task of unprecedented scale to any plant that may undertake it."

Despite the realization in 1940 that the war would not after all be brief, no one could know how long it would last. As early as 1943, the Mint was making preparations for the work which would follow once it ended. The medal unit was expanded and moved to better quarters. Space was found in the upper floor in the refinery's north wing. Light machinery capable of manufacturing both round and oval medals was moved in. This relieved pressure on the Mint machinery which was already fully occupied with the year's tremendous volume of coinage.

For the next two years, experimental medal work and considerable research in connection with equipment and organization were carried out in anticipation of the coming demand. Still the war had not ended, and only three war-related medals were produced.

The first was the Canada Medal, for "meritorious service above and beyond the faithful performance of duties," to be issued to eligible personnel of the armed forces or merchant navy as well as civilians of Canada or other countries. The obverse design was to carry the standard crowned effigy of King George VI. As a convenience, the Mint employed the die for the obverse of the Military Long Service Medal. The reverse, designed and engraved by Thomas Shingles, portrayed the Dominion Coat of Arms beneath a crown and surrounded by a wreath of maple leaves. Fourteen examples of this medal were struck in 1944 but were never awarded.

The second and third medals, the Military Long Service and Good Conduct Medal and the Canadian Efficiency Medal, were both for the Department of National Defence. Several hundred of the former and over eight thousand of the latter were produced between 1943 and 1946 from tools originating in England.

In 1945, with the war finally over, the Department of National Defence asked the Mint to prepare the master tools and produce service medals for Canada's armed forces. The contract stated that such work should not interfere with the essential production of coins. Originally medal production had been anticipated as a useful enterprise in the lull expected after the war. It now looked as if coinage demands would not fall at all, let alone enough for the Mint to undertake the enormous effort of producing the medals. As the Mint acknowledged, this work would "present a task of unprecedented scale to any plant that may undertake it."

Appropriate equipment for this special type of work was purchased from munitions plants which were being dismantled. These machines were carefully overhauled and repaired during the first half of 1946. The Medal Department was now further expanded and modernized. Special attention was given to the floor plan and colour scheme. The aim was to create a model plant for the manufacture of medals.

Work began in this new facility early in 1946 for the first of the four postwar medals, the Canadian Volunteer Service Medal. The design for the reverse was taken from a sketch by the Canadian Army Major, C.F. Comfort. This depicted a group of figures – representing the Navy, Army, Air Force and Nursing Service – marching on parade in the precision style developed in World War II. Surrounding the figures is a bilingual inscription set off with two maple leaves. The obverse carried the traditional Dominion Coat of Arms. The additional distinction of service overseas was indicated by attaching a bar bearing a maple leaf to the supporting ribbon.

The Medal Department concentrated on the production of this one medal. Anticipated production was 2,000 pieces per day, but technical problems at first prevented achievement of this level. Once they were overcome, two and one-half times the original goal could be attained if either the 250-ton coining press or one of three smaller ones could be spared from coining and adapted for striking medals. In this manner more than 139,000 of the required 900,000 Canadian Volunteer Service Medals were produced the first year despite the late starting time. The order was completed over the next two and a half years.

During that first postwar year, 1946, the Mint received a second request from the Department of National Defence, this time for 658,000 Campaign Stars. There were to be eight different designs, each representing a different campaign in which the Canadian Armed Forces had taken part. The greatest quantities would be required for those who had served from 1939 to 1945 and for veterans of action in France, Germany and Italy. Smaller quantities were required for those who had served in the Atlantic, in the "Aircrew Europe," in Africa, in Burma, and in the Pacific theatres.

The master tools for five of these stars were received from Britain by the end of 1946. The dies for all eight were prepared in time for at least some of each variety to be produced in 1947. All were struck in bronze. In all cases, service in more than one of the areas was distinguished by the addition of a bar to the ribbon as with the Volunteer Service Medal. In the case of the stars, the area of activity was inscribed on the bar. More than 266,000 stars and 25,000 bars were produced in 1947.

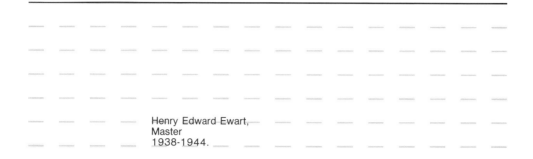

Henry Edward Ewart,
Master
1938-1944.

Thomas Shingles
engraving the reverse die for the
Canadian Volunteer Service Medal,
1945.
Malak.

Removing the burr from the edges of war medals,
1949.
Public Archives Canada PA-132083.

Assembling war medals,
1949
Public Archives Canada PA-132082.

"Despite the pressure, the order... was filled on time."

The following year saw nearly as great a volume, but only four kinds were struck. In 1949, the rest of the order was completed at the same time as the requirements for the Volunteer Service Medal. By the end of 1948, the Mint was approaching the conclusion of its existing medal contracts. The Defence Department now commissioned two different medals, the Defence of Britain Medal and the 1939-45 War Medal. In both cases, the most interesting feature is the reverse. The obverses were both traditional approved portraits of King George VI, the uncrowned effigy by Paget and the crowned by Metcalfe. The Defence of Britain Medal reverse featured an oak tree defended by a lion and lioness beneath the Imperial Crown. The War Medal portrayed a lion standing on a two-headed dragon. The two heads – an eagle's and a dragon's – signified the defeated Occidental and Asian enemies.

Although the matrices and punches for both medals were received from London in 1948, production did not begin until 1949. As mentioned before, demand for coins remained high even after the war, and the Mint was still working double and triple shifts. In addition, there were deadlines for the Volunteer Service Medals and the Campaign Stars. Despite the pressure, the order for 460,000 Defence of Britain medals and 1,060,000 War Medals was filled on time. All were struck in 800 fine silver. Both types were modelled in low relief so they could be struck at one blow on the heavy coining presses unlike the Volunteer Service Medal which required two or three blows.

15

The completion of the Defence Department orders, and the end of the pressure on the Medal Department occurred in September 1949, precisely ten years after Canada had gone to war and three years after the large-scale medal production had begun. Those three years had been every bit as hectic as the Acting Mint Master, A.P. Williams, had predicted in 1945. "A task of unprecedented scale," he had called it, and it had been just that; more than 3 million medals and stars had been struck as well as more than half a million bars as subsidiary awards. Often two or even three strikings per medal had been required. Presses had to be hand-fed. Clasps and ribbons and bars had to be attached. And everything had to be specially packaged.

The Mint's success in handling the task, combining artistic excellence with production efficiency, became obvious to the country when the presentation ceremonies took place in the autumn of 1949.

Britain Loses India Canada Gains Newfoundland

For the Royal Canadian Mint, the impact of the postwar years was not limited to the massive requirements for coinage and medals. The political structures of the world were in ferment. One great change was the granting of independence to India.

At first glance, this event, however momentous for India, might seem to have no relevance to the Mint. But since 1902, every Canadian coin had borne testimony to the reigning King's position as Emperor of India. Now the Royal Title INDIAE IMPERATOR, usually abbreviated IND: IMP: on coins, was no longer appropriate and the tools for making obverse dies had to be revised accordingly. The granting of independence to India in 1947 left the Mint with little opportunity to accumulate stocks of coins sufficient to provide for any delay in producing the new coins. Even if there had been advance warning, the Mint was too hard-pressed to do anything more than to meet current demands. Those demands also meant that there would be no question of simply waiting through several months of the new year until the matrices and punches arrived. Coins were too urgently needed. The only alternative was to continue striking with 1947-dated dies with their outmoded obverse legend, even though they were being used in 1948. This was the same solution the Mint had thought about in 1911, and actually resorted to in 1937.

Mohandas Gandhi
(1869-1948)

Nickel 5 cents,
1947,
from die marked with
a tiny maple leaf
after the date
to denote that it was
struck in 1948.

> *"Events thousands of miles away had once again exerted a significant effect on Canada's coinage."*

In the latter case, at least some of the antedated coins were identified with a small dot. Not all denominations were struck, and only one was issued in quantity. This was not the case in 1948. Starting early in the year, all denominations including the silver dollar were produced. The coins were marked this time with a tiny maple leaf placed after the date. The punch employed for this purpose is preserved in the National Currency Collection.

Perhaps because this alternative had been employed on all coins from the beginning of the year, the Royal Mint in London did not give Canada's new obverses special priority. The matrices and punches did not arrive in Ottawa until late in the year. Once in hand, they were immediately put to use. Thus there are at least some coins bearing the revised inscription and the 1948 date, but these generally make up a small percentage of the coins produced that year.

Events thousands of miles away had once again exerted a significant effect on Canada's coinage. The next change was very near at hand. Less than two years after India had gained its independence, Britain lost yet another portion of the Empire. Her oldest colony, Newfoundland, became Canada's tenth province. The move had been proposed as early as 1864 when the British North American colonies were debating Union, but Newfoundland had not joined. After the financial crisis of 1894, Confederation with Canada was again considered, but the terms offered by Ottawa were not sufficiently attractive. The colony recovered temporarily, but came to the brink of bankruptcy in the early 1930s. Self-government was replaced by a Commission of Government under a British-appointed governor.

Silver dollar obverses,
showing the legend changes that occurred
because India became independent.

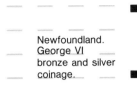
Newfoundland.
George VI
bronze and silver
coinage.

World War II presented clearly to both Canada and Newfoundland the advantages of union. After the fall of France in 1940, there was a growing sense of vulnerability. If Britain fell, both Canada and the United States would find themselves in close proximity to an unprotected land-mass. This realization led to the deployment of Canadian troops in Newfoundland. Airports were built to handle flights from North America to Britain via Greenland and Iceland. St. John's harbour was used heavily by British convoys.

Since 1940, the Royal Canadian Mint had been striking Newfoundland's coins in denominations of one, five and ten cents. At first the Mint was able to supply the colony's needs efficiently. However heavy Canadian demands which forced the Mint to work twenty-four hours a day, seven days a week, prevented until December the production of an order placed in June 1943. Further quantities of coins were shipped in 1944. Late that year, another supply of five- and ten-cent coins was ordered, the first for which Newfoundland agreed to accept the 800 fine silver alloy used for Canadian coins. Part of this order was shipped by the spring of 1945, but for the remainder Newfoundland was to endure a long delay.

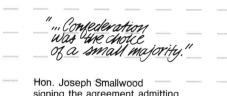

"... Confederation was the choice of a small majority."

Hon. Joseph Smallwood
signing the agreement admitting
Newfoundland into Confederation,
Ottawa, December, 1949.
Public Archives Canada PA-128080.

In 1946, the colony required more five-
and ten-cent coins which, hoping
for faster service, it ordered from
the Royal Mint in London. But the Royal
Mint was preparing to undertake a massive effort to replace Britain's 500 fine
silver coins by cupro-nickel pieces.
It suggested that Newfoundland should
continue to deal with Ottawa. Although
the Royal Canadian Mint received
the order late in 1946, it struck no coins
for Newfoundland that year. A shipment
was coined in January 1947, but
the coins it contained bore various dates
– 1947, 1946 and probably 1945.
The colony placed a final order which
was completed in September 1947, this
time for one- and ten-cent coins.

Meanwhile the matter of union with
Canada was being discussed. The
island's pro-Confederation activists, led
by Joseph Smallwood, managed
to secure attractive financial induce-
ments from Canada. In a referendum in June 1948, Newfoundlanders
had three choices: the extension
of the Commission of Government
for another five years; Confederation
with Canada; or self-government as
it existed before 1934. No option
received over fifty percent of the votes
so the alternative with the least support,
the Commission of Government, was
dropped. In a two-way referendum
the following month, Confederation was
the choice of a small majority.

To mark the official entry of Newfoundland
into Confederation at the end of March
1949, the Canadian Government authorized the issue of a commemorative silver
dollar, Canada's third. The design
selected was a whip under full sail representing the *"Matthew"* in which John
Cabot made his historic discovery
of Newfoundland in 1497, and the motto "FLOREAT TERRA NOVA" – "May
the new land flourish." The ship
design was taken from a photograph
of a model of the *"Matthew"* provided by Ernest Maunder of St. John's.
The same design was also used
on a postage stamp issued to commemorate the entry of Newfoundland
into Confederation.

Royal Canadian Mint Engraver Thomas
Shingles prepared the reverse master
tools from the photograph in only five
weeks, delicately cutting the matrix
in steel by hand. This was the second
coin to demonstrate his skill in this field.
The new obverse with the phrase ET
IND: IMP: deleted, was used. The coins
were struck from selected dies to give
them a superior finish, and most were
specially packaged in plastic tubes
to minimize "bag marks" and other
abrasions.

Walter Clifton Ronson,
Master,
1947-53.

Commemorative silver dollar for
Newfoundland's entry into Confederation,
1949.

16

The 1949 dollar was put into circulation
in late June. The first pieces were sent
to Newfoundland. The coin proved to be
a favourite, and the Mint planned
to strike it as long as it was in demand.
The dollar was so popular that more than
40,000 new pieces were required
in 1950, in addition to the 631,500
struck during the year 1949. Those
struck in 1950 retained the 1949 date.
The 1949 silver dollar is still considered
by many to be one of Canada's most
beautiful coins.

Updating the Mint

Physical conditions in the Mint during the 1940s had frequently verged on the nightmarish. The war years had been difficult enough, and postwar medal production, combined with continuing high pressure on the coinage facilities, resulted in even greater problems. The work areas grew ever more crowded and noisy. Although the building had not been significantly enlarged since its construction when it was judged suitable for a staff of 50 or 60, there were now more than 340 men and women employed. They worked in cramped quarters surrounded by the incessant clang and clatter of machines which were not only punching out coins but rattling from age. Most of the machines were more than forty years old and badly worn. In the melting room, the poorly-insulated furnaces drove the temperature to intolerable levels in summer, and were a constant source of danger.

The overcrowding resulted from the demand for coins, and although there was no indication during the late 1940s that the demand was growing greater, neither were there any signs that it was decreasing. R.J. Edmunds, Chief of the embattled Coining and Medal Division, assessed the situation in 1951:

"The Mint had been transformed from an institution which was still proving itself to one which was indispensable."

"Until recently the continued large scale orders for Canadian coinage, averaging about 100 million pieces annually over a period of twelve years, were considered abnormal and of temporary duration. In view of the changed condition and the consistent heavy demand for coin to meet the needs of the public, this average now has to be regarded as a normal year's production."

This was the great change which had come about during a war. The Mint had been transformed from an institution which was still proving itself to one which was indispensable. In the early 1950s, the first comprehensive study of the Mint since its establishment in 1908 recommended changes which would enable the plant to meet the now normal demands of 100 million pieces annually by working only one shift.

As a first step, the study recommended expansion to accommodate properly the existing personnel and equipment. Nevertheless, the expansion was not to be very great. The new area, south of the existing building but still connected to it, would house only coining presses. The small increase in floor area would free important space in the old building to allow more efficient disposition of other machinery, both old and new.

In the upgrading of the Mint facilities, the emphasis was to be on machines. Although working conditions would be improved for the employees, the main thrust was to reduce manpower by increasing the output per machine. Thus the new machines were chosen primarily on the basis of high-capacity performance. Many, if not all, of the old machines were improved.

This process of installing new equipment or upgrading existing machinery was to continue throughout the decade. The building program was completed much more quickly. Begun in 1950 and scheduled for completion in 1952, the new wing was only a few months late. The old coining presses, as well as a new one, were installed there in late 1953.

With the space problem solved, attention shifted to improving machine performance. By the end of the decade, every stage of the coining process from melting the alloys to examination of the finished coins had been worked on. In every case, the aim was to bring the capacity of a given stage up to the level of the stage with the highest capacity. At times, this might be in the coining room, at other times, the melting room or the cutting room. Each innovation in one phase inevitably put demands on its predecessor to supply more – metal bars, blanks or coin – or on its successor to handle more – in the blanking, coining or examining rooms.

The success of the overhaul was obvious. By the end of the decade, more than 132 million pieces were struck in one year. This quantity approached the record set in 1943, but was accomplished with far less strain. The alterations not only resulted in increased output but also permitted a reduction in manpower.

In the melting room, for instance, the new electric induction furnaces melted their charges in much less time than the old oil-fired furnaces without causing the work area to become uncomfortably hot. Furthermore they were larger. Each of these four furnaces replaced two of the previous models and eliminated the need for several workmen. Now this room could turn out more than three tons of bronze per normal working day. This was complemented by the development of new, large water-cooled moulds which yielded metal slabs of 175 pounds each, rather than the small bars produced previously.

To cope with the heavy slabs, the next stage, the rolling room was updated. Here, one large rolling unit replaced four smaller manually-fed mills. Its conveyors, occupying an area 72 feet long and 25 feet wide, delivered the slabs to the "roughing" mills, retrieved them after their first treatment and delivered them back again for another pass. In eleven passes, the ingots were compressed from 1.50 to .25 inches in thickness. At this gauge, they were ready for the faster "finishing" mills which further reduced the metal strip to the required gauge for coining. By this time, the slab, originally four feet long, had been stretched to 120 feet while the width remained just under eight inches.

These improvements in turn led to changes in the cutting room because the old methods could not keep pace with the increased production of metal strip. Again manual feed was replaced by mechanical feed. Furthermore the new mechanisms were two-sided so that one side was always in operation while the other was being loaded. These feeders delivered the strip to the cutting machines which included three new twenty-ton blank punches. All had been adapted to punch out several blanks at once. Vibrating screens were set up to automatically eliminate most of the incomplete blanks.[1] The screen was perforated with holes slightly smaller than the size of perfect blanks so that when shaken the defective blanks fell through.

The good blanks were quickly prepared for the coining presses by special automatic hoppers built at the Mint. These fed the blanks far more quickly than the old manual method (4,000 pieces per minute versus 1,400) to new high-speed edge-marking machines, also designed and built at the Mint. These blanks all received their final treatment before striking – softening – either in the old annealing furnaces, which had been enlarged, or in even faster modern equipment which once more reduced the amount of manual involvement. At the same time, the facilities in the press room and for producing dies had been vastly improved.

A highlight of the whole process of automating the Mint came when it acquired its own "reducing machine" made by Janvier of France. It was used to produce master tools from the artist's sculpted model, and eliminated most of the hand-engraving. Some maintained that the machine could not duplicate the delicacy of hand-cutting, but it was undeniably faster and that proved to be the determining factor.

Mint seen from the southeast.
The 1950-52 addition is at the left.
Public Archives Canada PA-132088.

"By the early 1950s, the Mint was equipped to handle efficiently the formidable workloads of the previous decade."

Now the Mint could not only make longer-lasting dies as a result of the chromium-plating process developed during World War II, but new dies could be produced in less time. The Mint Engraver would still hold an important position, but his tasks would be of a more refined and limited nature. As soon as possible, this machine and the engravers as well as the Medal and Machine Department were established in new headquarters. The work areas were now unified instead of being dispersed throughout the Mint building.

Renovations were next undertaken in the Press Room. Here, capacity was nearly doubled by the addition of five new presses and then the replacement of the seven original presses. A further increase in output of ten to twenty percent was achieved when all presses were equipped with automatic feeders as well as "single-lift" devices. The bottom dies formerly moved twice per cycle: first for striking and then to eject the coin. The new devices required the bottom dies to move only once. A conversion to alternating current again increased the production rate. Finally various safety devices made it possible for each operator to manage two machines rather than one so that manpower was again reduced.

To ensure that this increased volume and speed did not result in lower quality, the examining and telling facilities were improved. A second overlooking table was added as well as eight automatic weighing machines bringing the total number of weighing machines to twenty.

By the early 1950s, the Mint was equipped to handle efficiently the formidable workloads of the previous decade. Indeed it seemed possible at one point that the Mint had greater capacity than was needed, as was the case in 1908 and 1920. In 1954, the year the majority of the alterations were completed, coinage demands suddenly fell almost to pre-war levels. This marked the beginning of a period of relative calm at the Mint.

These years were not without their interest in terms of new coinage issues. The decade had its first new issue in 1951, the 200th anniversary of the discovery and naming of the element nickel by Swedish chemist A.F. Cronstedt. It was decided to commemorate this event on a Canadian coin. The logical denomination was the five cents, the only nickel coin in the Canadian series.

"His design ... was a tribute to the nickel industry in Canada."

This commemorative gesture was appropriate because of the role nickel had come to play in Canada's economic life. Since the first period of rapid development during the First World War, the country had become the world's largest producer of the metal accounting for over 90 percent of global production, 95 percent of which was exported. Canada, at the time, used the metal in only one of its denominations, but many other nations had replaced silver with nickel alloy coins.

In order to obtain the design for the reverse, a large and diverse design committee was appointed to oversee an open competition. This resulted in the unexpected submission of over 10,000 entries. Earlier committees had dealt with no more than 400 drawings.

The selected design was the work of Stephen Trenka, a Hungarian-born engraver who had emigrated to Canada and studied at the Ontario College of Art. His design depicting a nickel refinery was a tribute to the nickel industry in Canada. Official announcement of the winning entry was made during a ceremony at the Mint on December 18, 1950, in the presence of representatives from the International Nickel Company and the Falconbridge Nickel Company.

The reverse bore the dual dates 1751-1951. Many people, under the misapprehension that the first date was incorrect and should read 1851, hoarded the coins thinking they would become valuable rarities when the supposed error was corrected.

The 1951 commemorative five-cent piece did very nearly become scarce. The Korean War which had begun in the summer of 1950 put renewed pressure on Canada's supply of refined nickel which was useful for weapons of war as well as for coins. Once again the five-cent piece had to be composed of steel. This time it was coated with a very thin (.01 mm) layer of nickel and plated with chromium. The regular beaver reverse with very slight modifications was used again. Only the Mint's early production, beginning in 1950, of more than eight million commemorative coins saved the country from having to honour the discovery of nickel with a steel coin. It also deprived speculators of a rarity.

The remaining coinage changes to occur during the decade deserve a chapter of their own.

Commemorative nickel five cents, 1951.

Steel five cents, 1951.

17

Note:

[1] Such blanks, which have a flat spot along the edge instead of being perfectly round, come from the strip ends.

A New Queen
Graces Our Coins

The coronation of the new Queen, Elizabeth II, was a highlight of the 1950s. She succeeded to the throne on February 6, 1952, upon the death of her father, King George VI. In accordance with past practices, coins could continue to be struck throughout 1952 in the name of the late King. New obverse dies would not be required until 1953. There appeared to be adequate time to prepare for the coinage of the new reign, but it remained to be seen whether anything would occur to jeopardize the process as it had in 1936. The Royal Mint faced a mammoth task preparing master tools for the mints in Pretoria, Perth, Melbourne and Ottawa as well as for London's Tower Hill, and new coinages for the other countries of the Commonwealth.

The crucial first step was to select the obverse effigy. In the search for the best possible portrait, new artists as well as the acknowledged masters were consulted. This approach had already proven useful in obtaining reverse designs. On this occasion, a total of seventeen plaster models were received, all sculpted from profile photographs of Her Majesty.

Queen Elizabeth II
wearing her coronation robes
and the Imperial State Crown, 1953.
Public Archives Canada PA-18846.

> *"But when the new dies were put into the coinage presses, problems arose."*

Initial silver dollar obverse, 1953.

For the uncrowned portrait to be used by Canada, as well as by Southern Rhodesia, Australia, New Zealand, South Africa and Great Britain, the Royal Mint Advisory Committee under the Presidency of His Royal Highness the Duke of Edinburgh chose the submission by Mrs. Mary Gillick. The sculptress, then in her seventieth year, was granted personal sittings with Her Majesty. This enabled her to complete the obverse portrait at an early date.

For the first time, Britain and Canada agreed that Canada would produce its own obverse master tools direct from the artist's model. Thus more than forty years after Dr. Bonar complained that Canada should be able to make her own die-sinking tools, that goal was realized. Meanwhile the other Dominions with their own mints, Australia and South Africa, still had to wait on Britain.

The Royal Mint displayed its confidence in its former branch by sending to Ottawa a model without inscription. Royal Canadian Mint technicians produced from it a second plaster model in intaglio into which the inscription was cut. Two sets of intermediate models were made; one was set aside in case the other was damaged.

All steps had been completed and, in fact, some obverse dies had actually been sunk before the end of 1952, six months in advance of the Coronation. For the first time, the Mint actually appeared ready to produce new coinage without delay. But when the new dies were put into the coinage presses, problems arose. The relief of the Queen's portrait was slightly higher than that on the previous issue. The coins were consequently harder to strike, and the details in the highest areas were indistinct. Similar difficulties were encountered by all Mints.

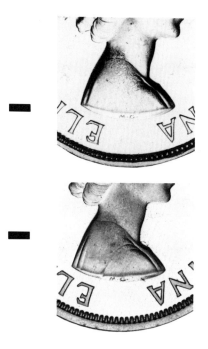

Initial high relief and revised lower relief silver dollar obverses, 1953.

"Small date" and "large date"
50-cent reverses,
1953.

While the other countries suffered
for some time with the defective
obverses, Canada was quick to deal
with the problem. Thomas Shingles,
the Royal Canadian Mint's Chief
Engraver and a master at miniature
engraving, was able to make the cor-
rections quickly. The intermediate
model was adjusted to lower the relief,
and the Queen's hair, laurel wreath
and gown details were skillfully and
tastefully retouched. Other adjustments
were made on punches for individual
denominations. The coin diameter was
slightly increased for both the twenty-
five-cent piece and silver dollar to permit a wider rim.

A generally satisfactory result was
achieved with all denominations except
the fifty-cent piece. This coin required
such a large amount of metal to bring
up the portrait that the reverse did
not strike up properly. Minor adjustment of the date size and position
of the reverse design did not eliminate the problem which was not
finally solved until the whole reverse
design was rendered significantly
smaller in 1955.

The fifty-cent piece underwent a more
dramatic alteration in 1959. A change
of the Canadian Coat of Arms required
a wholesale revision of the reverse
design.

Shingles modelled and engraved the new
design and substituted, at the suggestion of The Queen, the St. Edward's
Crown for the Imperial Crown.

Revised fifty-cent reverse
(e.g. smaller shield),
1955.

Reverse for fifty-cent piece
with the newly-adopted coat of arms,
1959.

British Columbia
commemorative
silver dollar,
1958.

Meanwhile a new commemorative silver dollar had been issued in 1958 to mark the centenary of the Caribou Gold Rush and the establishment of British Columbia as a Crown Colony. Again a design by Stephen Trenka won the competition. His attractive submission featured a totem pole against a background of mountains.

There was, however, some controversy regarding the suitability of the design. On the one hand, it made no direct reference to the Gold Rush, while on the other, it drew attention to native peoples who had nothing to do with the establishment of British Columbia as a Crown Colony. In fact, the West Coast Indians rejected the coin since in their mythology the raven at the top represented death.

Totem poles,
Alert Bay, British Columbia,
ca. 1910.
Pubilc Archives Canada PA-60023.

Bronze Coronation medal, 1953.

Despite such concerns, more than three million of these coins were produced, almost ten times the usual number and three times the record set by the 1939 commemorative. More than one third went to British Columbia where mining interests had long supported the coinage of silver dollars.

The Medal Section was also active in the 1950s. Britain had been disappointed by the response to the medal it had struck for the Coronation of King George VI. Therefore it did not plan a medal to commemorate the Coronation of Queen Elizabeth II. Canada, which had marketed the British medal in 1937, decided to create one of its own.

Since Britain was not producing a medal, Canada had more than the usual freedom of choice in the matter of selecting a suitable obverse. Twenty-seven possibilities had been prepared in Britain by individual designers and firms, and passed on to the Official Coronation Medal Panel. From these the Royal Mint Advisory Committee had chosen one for which it was willing to furnish dies. Canada, despite its freedom, chose this alternative valuing the convenience as much as the design.

The portrait was modelled by Mr. G.H. Paulin of London. It showed Queen Elizabeth crowned and robed, facing right. It was distinctive for its lack of surrounding inscription. An inscription surrounding the Royal Cypher surmounted by the St. Edward's Crown was included on the reverse. The whole of the reverse was modelled by the Mint engraver.

Unlike the procedure for the Royal Tour of 1939, no gold or silver presentation pieces were struck, but more than three million bronze medals were made for school children.

The Medal Section was awarded many contracts for other medals. Even before the war medals were finished, two new pieces were prepared for the Engineering Institute bringing its total to seven different kinds. The Mint had also produced the Governor General's medals for education and one each for the Professional Institute of the Canadian Civil Service and for the National Fitness Award. The latter was first presented to Barbara Ann Scott, Canada's skating champion.

In the year after completion of the war contracts, a medal was created for the Art Directors' Club, an example of which was awarded to the artist, Harold Town; the Royal Architecture Institute commissioned a medal, and there was even a Royal Canadian Mint Long Service Medal of which eight were presented.

"Suddenly, in early 1960, the level of Mint activity began to change."

In 1951, the Chemical Institute of Canada commissioned eight medals for presentation to staff of the International Nickel Company. The obverse featured the scientist Cronstedt whose isolation of nickel in 1751 had been commemorated on the five-cent piece. The reverse bore the monogram of the Chemical Institute of Canada. Other distinctive pieces included the John Howard Humanitarian Medal and the Royal Canadian Geographical Society's Medal. By the end of the decade, the Medal Section had cut dies for and/or struck more than fifty types of medals, most to be produced on an annual basis.

The success in the Medal Section was in keeping with that throughout the Mint – renovations had been completed and coinage demands and changes handled effectively. Suddenly in early 1960, the level of Mint activity began to change. Soon demand would exceed all previous records and make the planning of the 1950s seen shortsighted. The facilities, which only the year before had easily coped with an impressive 132 million pieces, now had to struggle to handle a new record production of 182 million pieces.

There was no obvious explanation for the increase – no commemoratives, no new issues, no special events – just enormous demands for coin. The increase in that particular year did not apply so much to the cent as to the five-, ten- and twenty-five-cent denominations. The trend continued in 1961, when more than 237 million coins were struck. At this point, the total was double the capacity for which the Mint had so recently been designed. Demand was never again to fall below the 200 million mark; indeed, each of the next three years was to set a new, short-lived record of production. Clearly a new era had begun.

In 1958, after the Mint's first fifty years of operation, the amount of change in circulation averaged just over $8.00 per person. By the end of 1964, a year which saw an astonishing 665 million coins produced, the figure had jumped to over $13.00 for every Canadian.

How could a plant, streamlined in the 1950s to handle an annual output of 100 million pieces, possibly be responsible for more than six times that many? Certainly some of the increase in volume could be accomplished by working around the clock rather than a single shift. However such an answer would mean new problems in bookkeeping, security and mechanical maintenance.

Another obstacle to a simple solution to the increasing pressure was uncertainty about how long it would last. There were no guarantees that the new level of demand would be permanent. Experience did not offer any insights. So from the onset of the demands of the 1960s, the attempts to cope looked more like the frantic scramble of the war years than the orderly planning of the 1950s.

At first, the Mint relied on a combination of more machines and more personnel to cope with its increased volume of business. No matter how extensive the changes in the Mint's half-dozen departments, the scene of the greatest activity was always in actual coin production. More presses, larger and faster than the older models, were added. The growth was so rapid that there was hardly time to prepare adequate accommodation for the new machinery. Most additional presses were hastily installed in the basement of the 1961 extension which came to be known as "the new press room."

At the same time, improvements were made in the cutting room. Four straighteners were installed to smooth out coiled strip quickly and uniformly. Other facilities were provided for bulk handling of strip. A new 50-ton press to cut blanks was installed, together with additional equipment for annealling, cleaning and drying blanks.

Alfred Percy Williams, Master 1954-1959.

Although progress had been made earlier in extending the life of individual dies, these advances had not kept pace with the recent abrupt increase in coinage output. Only virtually indestructible dies, capable of many, many more impressions than existing dies, could have prevented an increase in die consumption. Since this was not possible, vastly increased numbers of dies had to be turned out.

A major breakthrough was made in 1965 when the recently-established Engineering Division, responsible for machinery in the plant, developed an improved technique for die production. It permitted dies to be produced more quickly while reducing the need for highly-trained personnel.

In other areas though, new machinery required additional staff further adding to the chaos and congestion in the plant. Since the 1940s, there had been about 200 employees; by 1962, there were 274, and by 1965, 360.

Machinery and people were essential to the Mint's success during these difficult years, but they were not enough on their own. The country's coinage requirements were only met by the Mint relinquishing part of its self-sufficiency.

Until 1964, the Mint had directly controlled all aspects of coinage from the preparation of its coinage alloys to the striking of its coins. The only exception was the purchase from commercial sources of nickel strip for the five-cent coins. The reliance upon commercial suppliers was in 1964 extended to the bronze strip for the cent. This development greatly reduced the pressure on the melting and rolling sections freeing some staff to take up work in the press room. It also reduced the need for technical innovations in these areas, and allowed the energy for improvement to be focussed on a smaller number of functions.

Major Coinage Changes in the 1960s

Despite the heavy coinage demands that began in 1960 and the somewhat frantic efforts required to meet them, the Mint paid careful attention to the design of its coins. This period came to be characterized by very extensive changes in all denominations.

The first change was more a matter of necessity than choice. In particular, the five-cent piece went through yet another transformation prompted by technical considerations. The problem was that its distinctive twelve-sided shape, introduced in 1942 to help people distinguish between the brass five-cent piece and the bronze cent, created production difficulties when the composition reverted to nickel. The combination of the unusual shape and the notoriously hard nickel was extremely damaging to the collars which tended to crack at the corners. This had already aroused some concern, but now, with time at a premium and an ever-increasing demand for five-cent pieces, it became intolerable. Neither the time lost due to frequent collars' changes and the manufacture of new collars nor the cost for staff time and materials could be borne any longer. Late in 1962, a proclamation was issued to authorize in the new year the production of the first round five-cent coins since 1942.

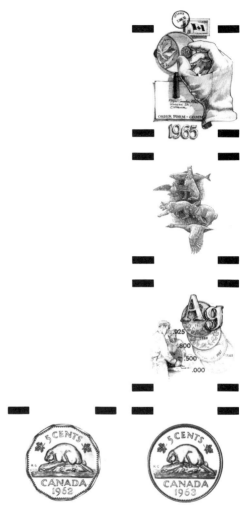

Nickel five-cent pieces,
12-sided,
1962,
and round,
1963.

A more artistic change occurred in 1964. Canada issued the fifth in its series of commemorative silver dollars. This coin recalled the conferences held at Charlottetown, P.E.I. and Quebec City one hundred years earlier which had led to Confederation. The design competition had been launched well in advance, during 1962, by Finance Minister Donald Fleming. The first prize of $1000 was awarded to Mr. Dinko Vodanovic of Montreal. His sketch for the reverse depicted, within a circle, emblems of four of the country's founding ethnic groups – French, Irish, Scottish and English – and surrounded the circle with an appropriate inscription. The reverse also bore the initials of the designer and of Thomas Shingles, who prepared the model. Shingles retired, after twenty-five years of service, as Chief Mint Engraver in the same year. Although the design was not admired as much as those of the earlier commemoratives, the coin was so much in demand that well over seven million pieces were struck.

Commemorative silver dollar
for Confederation conferences,
1964.

Delegates to the Confederation conference in Charlottetown, P.E.I.,
1864.
Public Archives Canada C-12169.

"The Royal Mint ... produced a new effigy more in keeping with the monarch's contemporary appearance."

The year 1964 was important for Canadian coinage in another way. The Royal Mint, in consultation with the Queen, produced a new effigy more in keeping with the monarch's contemporary appearance. The British artist and sculptor, Arnold Machin, was commissioned to produce the model. The design he submitted was distinctive not only for the more mature features of the Queen, but for the more elaborate gown and jewelled tiara which she wore. This effigy occupied a larger area on the coin than the former portrait, and was surrounded by a revised legend in which the formal DEI GRATIA was reduced to D.G. It was introduced on Canadian coinage in 1965.

"Mature" coinage obverse.
introduced in 1965.

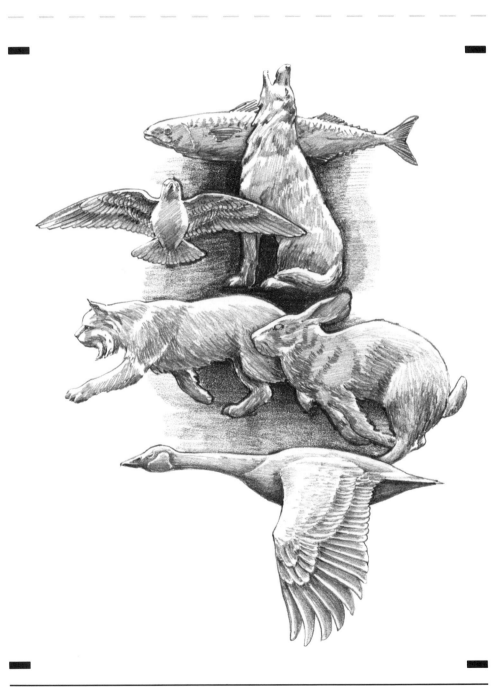

" In 1964 the Minister of Finance announced a design competition."

The highlight of coinage design changes in the 1960s came in connection with the celebration of the 100th anniversary of the Confederation of 1867 which had created the Dominion of Canada. In 1964, the Minister of Finance announced a design competition for a set of six new reverses for the cent through dollar denominations to be issued during the centennial year. It was open to all artists, sculptors and designers residing in Canada, and to Canadians living elsewhere. Unlike the initial competition of this kind held in 1927, this contest was planned well in advance. The deadline for design submissions was March 31, 1965.

Both the size of the award ($2,500) and the composition of the panel of judges testified to the importance given the new designs.

Confederation commemorative coinage, 1967, including a gold $20, Canada's first gold coin since 1914.

Norval Alexander Parker,
Master 1959-1968.

*"All denominations featured
common varieties of
Canadian wildlife..."*

Mint Master Norval A. Parker chaired
the panel. He was joined by prominent
designers and graphic artists as well
as two sculptors and a noted numisma-
tist, the late J. Douglas Ferguson. This
group finally selected the designs submitted by Alex Colville, the New
Brunswick artist and sculptor.

All denominations featured common
varieties of Canadian wildlife, and
avoided symbols which had perhaps
been overworked previously. The rock
dove associated with spiritual values
and peace was chosen for the one
cent; a rabbit connected with fertility,
new life and promise, for the five cent;
the mackerel symbol of continuity,
for the ten cent; a prowling bobcat
expressing intelligent independence and
decisive action, for the twenty-five cent;
a howling wolf symbolic of the vastness
and loneliness of Canada, for the fifty
cent; and the Canada goose with its
serene dynamic quality, for the silver
dollar.

After some discussion, the pre-1967
designs were restored in 1968. Particularly strong preference was expressed
for the schooner ten-cent piece widely
believed to portray the highly-revered
"Bluenose".

The enterprise directed towards these
changes was also applied to the numismatic or collectors' coins offered for sale
by the Mint. The superior quality of these
coins made them attractive to collectors
and investors alike.

In 1960, the same year which saw
the start of the dramatic increases
in domestic coinage demands, there
was also an impressive rise in the number of orders for numismatic coins.
The number of sets issued more than
doubled, although the distribution
of single dollars only rose 30 percent.
Two years after this, the demand
encouraged partly by speculation was
so great that by August the Mint had
to refuse further requests. Even so
more than 200,000 sets and nearly
48,000 dollars were sold that year.
Still the demand spiralled upwards.
In 1963, orders rose to 673,000 sets
and nearly 250,000 one-dollar coins.

During this time, little had been done
to increase the facilities of the Numismatic Section. The larger volume had
primarily been handled by adding extra
staff and working longer hours. In 1960,
a special coin-packing device had been
designed and built at the Mint to seal
each coin set in a flat pliofilm pouch.
And in 1963, a machine had been purchased to insert each coin set, together
with relevant enclosures, into a protective envelope for shipping.

In 1964, with domestic demands at their
peak, orders for numismatic coins were
cut off in April. But filling those already
received produced yet another record:
1.6 million sets and 1.2 million dollars.
This was sixteen times as many sets,
and sixty times as many dollars as four
years earlier! Two of the Mint's twenty
presses were fully occupied just meeting
this specialized demand.

This demand for numismatic coins meant that the Mint's ability to produce coins for general circulation was in serious danger of being hampered. Consequently for its 1965 numismatic programme, the Mint imposed new rules to minimize pressure on its overloaded facilities. Sets would be sold at a higher price, with a limit of five sets per person and a maximum production of two million sets. Moreover no separate silver dollars would be available.

The result of these precautions was far from what had been anticipated. Instead of eliminating the problem, they seemed to aggravate it. Such a limited production, coupled with high demand, clearly suggested that those who were able to obtain the 1965 collector's coins directly from the Mint stood to make a substantial profit in reselling them later.

As 1964 drew to a close, hopeful speculators descended upon Ottawa, aware that the Mint would not accept orders postmarked before January 1. Many carried orders for non-collector friends; others had orders using fictitious names and the true sender's address. At the stroke of midnight, the envelopes went into the mail slots of the postal terminal nearest to the Mint.

On January 2, its first day of business in the new year, the Mint received the startling news from the post office: a veritable mountain of orders had already arrived and there was no sign of a let-up. In fact, the limit of two million sets was reached on that first day and the Mint was forced to return orders for an estimated additional four million sets. This represented a substantial amount of lost revenue.

The 1965 numismatic coin situation was deemed sufficiently important to receive parliamentary attention. Following some discussion, the Finance Minister announced that the acceptance of orders for the 1965 sets would be resumed. All orders would be filled, no matter how much time was required. It was also decided to expand the Numismatic Section and transfer it to larger quarters outside the Ottawa plant in order to cope with the burgeoning demand.

Expansion of the section was swift and effective. Premises were located at the Government's Printing Bureau building across the Ottawa River in Hull, Quebec. Four presses were installed and production began. The new facility had a capacity of three million sets per year on a single-shift basis. Blanks for the process still had to come from Ottawa, and administrative control also remained there, but production and packaging were now distinctly separate.

1965

The effect of these measures on the speculators was devastating. Since no limit was to be imposed on production, there was no reason to pay a high price for those sets already on the open market. Prices plummetted. The speculative bubble, which had been extended to rolls and even mint-sealed bags of new circulating coins, had clearly burst. With the hope of easy profits gone, the sets seemed to lose much of their appeal. Less than a million additional 1965 sets were ordered after requests began to be accepted again.

The Centennial year 1967 offered the Mint an opportunity to undertake its most ambitious numismatic project up to that time. Three kinds of sets of the new-design coins were offered to collectors: the familiar six-coin set in plastic, a set in a red leather-covered case (containing a sterling silver medallion in addition to the standard six coins), and a "gold set" in a black leather-covered case. The gold set contained the cent through the dollar and a twenty-dollar gold coin bearing Canada's coat of arms on its reverse. All coins that went into the gold set were of the best quality that the Mint could then produce. Some sets even had lacquered coins, to help ensure that their beautiful finish would remain free of tarnish for many years.

Despite the various changes to the shape, appearance and quantity of Canada's coins, the outstanding alteration during this period concerned the composition of the coins. The silver content of 80 percent in the ten cents through dollar represented a notable amount of precious metal. During the 1960s, it proved to be too much.

If the price of silver reached $1.66 per ounce Troy, the bullion value in Canadian silver coins would equal their face value. Although silver sold for less than $1.00 per ounce in 1960, production was not keeping up with consumption. A sudden sharp price increase was a distinct possibility. For speculators, this prospect held out the possibility of gain. For the Mint, it posed a huge threat. In view of the high volume produced, coining carried out at a loss would prove to be tremendously expensive.

By 1964, silver reserves held by the United States Treasury had fallen to half the level of six years earlier. Although the Treasury was still selling silver at $1.29 per ounce, it was anticipated that the price would soon be allowed to float to whatever level the market would bear. With this possibility in mind, the Mint recommended to the Finance Department in September 1964 that Canada follow the example of the United Kingdom in switching to cupro-nickel, and that it be done by 1966.

"The delay quickly became crucial."

The Finance Department gave the suggestion serious consideration and studied the problem. The Mint was asked to submit a memorandum on moves away from silver by other countries. Mint Master Norval Parker visited the United States to appraise the situation there. Parker found that tests for a replacement for silver were being conducted, and that the United States expected to make the transition very soon.

Nevertheless Canada took no decisive action. The Mint conducted experiments on various alternative metals, including cupro-nickel. But it was not until 1966, the year originally proposed for the transition, that a government committee was formed to decide on a new coinage alloy. They quickly reached a conclusion: of five possible substitutes for silver, pure nickel was the best on the basis of appearance, availability, distinctiveness from U.S. coins and compatibility with Mint techniques.

In 1967, the Finance Minister gave notice that the Currency Act would be changed, and announced a target date of early 1968 for the transition. The length of time was based on one principal factor. Nickel was not compatible with Canada's vending machines. If the Mint were suddenly to produce a coinage which no longer operated the machines, the industry would experience considerable hardship. The only reasonable course was to allow time for the development and installation of selection mechanisms which would accept nickel coins.

The delay quickly became crucial. By the early summer of 1967, the United States had produced enough of its new cupro-nickel clad coins to replace every silver coin in the country. The government no longer had to hold down the price of silver which jumped from $1.30 to as much as $2.17 per ounce. Suddenly, 1968 was no longer a safe date for Canada's transition; it was at least a year too late. Immediate action was needed.

It was decided to reduce the silver content to 50 percent which would leave the Mint with some profit margin without interfering with the operation of the existing vending machines.

In September of 1967, the decision was made to cease production of the silver dollar and fifty cent denominations in an attempt to meet the great demand for ten- and twenty-five-cent coins. Only the latter two denominations were struck with the reduced silver content in that year. Yet the new 50 percent silver coins barely allowed the Mint to cover the expense of their production because silver rose to $2.56 per ounce. The immediate introduction of pure nickel on the other hand would have resulted in great profit. The government lost additional money when it yielded to industry pressure and agreed to compensate the vending machine companies for the expense of purchasing new selector mechanisms. The cost per machine was not great since the five new devices offered on the market were all priced at under twenty dollars. But given the total number of machines involved, this represented a significant expense to the Government of Canada.

Some resolution to the problem was essential if the change to nickel coinage was ever to be made. In the interim, more and more opportunity for profit on coinage issue was being lost.

The transition finally occurred part way through the production of coinage for 1968. In the early part of the year, the only silver coins struck for circulation were ten- and twenty-five-cent pieces

in .500 fine silver. Despite the concentration on these denominations, it was not possible to keep up with the demand because silver coins were being hoarded by speculators.

The new nickel coins were finally authorized for August 1968. They were somewhat darker and less brilliant than their silver predecessors, but they were accepted by the general public. Partly in an attempt to save money, the dollar and fifty-cent coins were substantially reduced in size. To strike nickel coins in the old sizes would have meant unacceptable die consumption. Dies

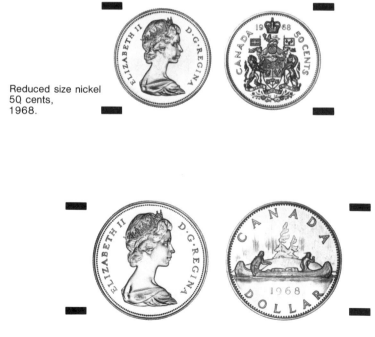

Reduced size nickel
50 cents,
1968.

Reduced size nickel $1,
1968.

for larger diameter coins wore faster; moreover, the dramatic rise in die use resulting from the greater hardness of nickel (compared to silver) was going to be difficult enough to accept.

The year 1968 also marked the first time since the opening of the Mint that an order for domestic coinage was placed with a foreign government. Specifically 85 million ten cent coins were ordered from the Philadelphia Branch of the U.S. Mint. Hoarding had developed to such an extent that the Royal Canadian Mint could not produce the new coins fast enough to accommodate the transition. Naturally the imported coins were purchased at greater cost than if they had been produced in Canada.

One of the greatest changes resulting from the switch in metals occurred in the Mint itself. Immediately there was a great reduction in the activity of the Melting and Rolling Departments. Most of the plant's needs were purchased as finished blanks which required only final striking to convert them into money. There was some possibility that this was only a temporary condition, and there was talk of carrying out more of the preliminary stages as time went on. But it seemed likely that for some time to come, the metal would be obtained in the form of strip. Complete Mint control over all phases of coin production was clearly a thing of the past.

19

The Change to a Crown Corporation

The sudden and shifting coinage demands from 1960 onwards brought a need for streamlining the Mint's administration. Some progress had been made in this area by a realignment of personnel in 1965. In the first reorganization in over a decade, the Mint Office was separated into Financial and Administrative Divisions.

But such internal restructuring was not enough. The bureaucratic link between the Mint and the government bodies which controlled it — the Finance Department and the Treasury Board — remained painfully awkward. In particular, neither additional manpower nor emergency funds could ever be obtained with sufficient speed to adapt to the rapidly changing conditions of the decade.

The internal administrative changes in 1965, combined with the retirement of a substantial number of senior personnel, required the rapid recruitment of many new managers. Unfortunately the authorization for hiring was slow in coming. The Mint simply did not have the authority to respond quickly enough to the problems it was facing.

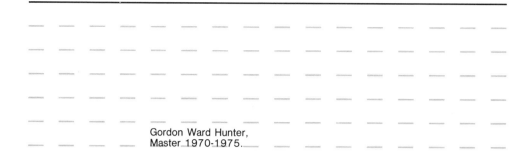

Gordon Ward Hunter,
Master 1970-1975.

" ... the Mint should be made a Crown Corporation."

This problem suggested that it might be better to grant the Mint greater authority by making it a Crown Corporation. This solution was given serious consideration as early as September 1964. However nothing specific was done until the terrible strain during the transition from silver to nickel made it impossible to overlook the need for change. A group was quickly appointed to examine the situation and advised that the Mint should be made a Crown Corporation. That summer, the government gave formal approval and began preparation of the required legislation. On April 1, 1969, the Mint became a Crown Corporation.

Almost half a century earlier, Finance Minister W.S. Fielding declined to assume control of the Mint claiming it was beyond his domain and expertise. Now the control had finally passed to the Mint's own officials, including an experienced, business-oriented Board of Directors immediately familiar with its needs and concerns.

The mandate for the Crown Corporation specifically encouraged the Board to direct the Mint in anticipation of profit. No longer would it be enough for the Mint simply to supply a needed commodity.

The goal of achieving a favourable balance sheet presented a challenge. The new Crown Corporation had been established to cope more efficiently with unprecedented coinage demands. Instead it faced declining volume. As had been the case throughout the century, little could be done to stimulate domestic coinage demand, the principal source of Mint income. One expedient previously resorted to, the exportation of American coin, would not serve in this case because U.S. coin had effectively been driven out of circulation when the Canadian dollar was devalued in 1962. The redemption of worn and mutilated coin, which had created Mint activity in 1909, was not a useful option either. The country's nickel coinage was still quite new, and the silver coinage was rapidly disappearing into the hands of speculators and collectors.

If profit was to be made, the Corporation had to look to new products – coins for foreign countries and coins for collectors, both foreign and domestic. Foreign markets promised the greater rewards. More than one hundred countries in the world had circulating coinages, but of these only forty had their own mints. The rest relied on foreign suppliers. Only ten mints in the world could handle outside requirements; the others were only large enough to meet their own country's needs.

Encouraged by these figures, the Royal Canadian Mint sought to enter the foreign coin market. It had, of course, already handled orders for Newfoundland, Jamaica and the Dominican Republic decades earlier. During the Second World War, it had again shown a willingness to take on new orders by entering into long negotiations for a contract with Nicaragua. Only the difficulties of acquiring the highly sought-after cupro-nickel during the war prevented the undertaking of this contract.

Pleased with its past successes and confident in its own vast mineral resources, Canada actively sought contracts. It hoped to capture 20 percent of the world market, a target which would demand the production of approximately 500 million coins.

In the summer of 1969, only four months after the establishment of the Crown Corporation, it appeared that Canada might soon be producing coins for Greece. Serious study of that country's requirements and of Canada's ability to handle them went ahead rapidly. Unfortunately this early opportunity proved impractical because certain conditions of the contract, including the need to weigh every coin separately, seemed to make it a liability.

But other opportunities quickly followed. In 1970, the Corporation was successful in winning contracts for the supply of six million cupro-nickel blanks for Singapore and 84 million more for the Central Bank of Brazil. The first coinage orders soon followed consisting of "5 fils" coins for the People's Republic of Yemen and "1 krona" coins for the Republic of Iceland. These advances were consolidated in 1972 when the output of foreign coins rose to over 100 million pieces, including a large and important order for Venezuela.

The future looked bright indeed, and such successes were paralleled by developments in the Numismatic Division. The speculative ardour for uncirculated sets had cooled when Finance Minister Walter Gordon decided to supply as many 1965 sets as the public wanted. Orders declined considerably in 1966. Although there was some recovery in 1967 sparked by interest in the special commemorative coins of that year, the demand continued to abate in 1968 and 1969 with the conversion to nickel coins. Not only did these latter sets lack silver coins, they were also of inferior quality, as the Mint struggled to find economical ways to impart a pleasing finish to the troublesome nickel coins. By 1970, the problem was solved and the coin sets for that year were much improved.

Iceland.
Nickel-brass 1 krona,
1971.

Yemen.
Bronze 5 fils,
1971.

Jamaica.
Gold $20,
1972.

The next step was a marketing campaign to increase numismatic sales. The product line was diversified. In 1971, two new seven-coin sets in attractive cases were introduced. The less expensive "custom" set had two one cent pieces whereas the "prestige" set had two nickel dollars. The extra coin in each showed the obverse (head side).

"Prestige" collectors' coin set with two nickel dollars, 1971.

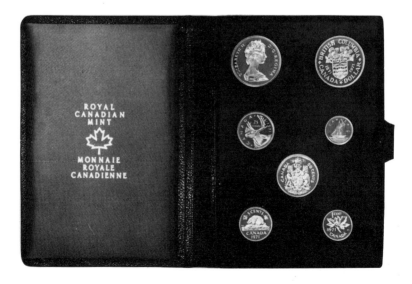

The most important numismatic development of 1971, however, did not concern the coin sets. Public opinion samples revealed that collectors had been much saddened by the demise of the silver dollar series in 1967. Consequently a .500 fine silver dollar in the old size was reinstituted in 1971. Unlike its .800 fine predecessors, it was intended strictly as a collectors' coin. It cost significantly more to produce than its face value and was available only at a premium.

"Custom" collectors' coin set with two one-cent pieces, 1971.

An interesting question was raised by the "new" silver dollar series: would the designs of the silver and smaller nickel dollars be the same? For several years, the coins reflected a degree of uncertainty. In 1971, both the silver and nickel dollars marked the centennial of British Columbia's entry into Confederation. But the designs, the work of separate artists, were completely different. In 1972, both coins bore the standard Voyageur reverse. However in 1973, the nickel dollar commemorated the hundredth anniversary of Prince Edward Island's entry into Confederation, while the silver dollar (and, surprisingly, the twenty-five-cent piece) paid tribute to the hundredth anniversary of the Royal Canadian Mounted Police.

The dollar coins for 1974 presented another possible combination. Both the nickel and silver versions bore identical reverse designs for the centennial of the City of Winnipeg. This practice was found undesirable from a sales standpoint, so, beginning in 1975, the silver dollar carried a commemorative design, while its nickel counterpart usually received the Voyageur design (but in any case, not the same design as the silver dollar).

Commemorative. 500 fine silver dollars for collectors,
1971, 1973-75.

Commemorative nickel dollars,
1970, 1971, 1973 and 1974.

"... *coins for the Olympic Games to be held in Montreal in 1976.*"

Packaging Olympic proof sets, 1974.

In 1973, the Numismatic Division became involved in a much more ambitious project. This was the production of coins for the Olympic Games to be held in Montreal in 1976. The coins were to be sold to raise money to defray the cost of staging the Games. Indeed the Olympic Committee optimistically maintained that the coin sales would entirely pay for the Games.[1]

The initial meetings were held at the Mint in February of 1973. Even then, time was pressing if design and production were to be carried out early enough. The first-ever Canadian Olympic coins were to consist of seven thematic[2] sets of four .925 fine silver coins (two $5 and two $10) for a total of twenty-eight coins and a $100 gold coin.

Gold $100 Olympic coin, 1976.

The design requirements for the silver coins were somewhat unusual. All would have a common obverse, Machin's portrait of Queen Elizabeth. The reverses would be different only in some respects. Almost half the space was taken up by the Olympic symbol, the denomination and the wording. These always occupied the same positions. The main design element, therefore, was restricted to a horizontal area at the lower centre. Another unusual aspect of these coins was that the lettering and sometimes even the design were essentially two-dimensional. These details were added not by conventional engraving but by photochemical etching.

The issue of the seven series of silver coins was scheduled to begin with series I in late 1973 and end with series VII just prior to the opening of the Olympics in 1976. By August 1973, all four designs for the first series were ready and, the following month, numerous staff were taken on to cope with the enormous demands of production.

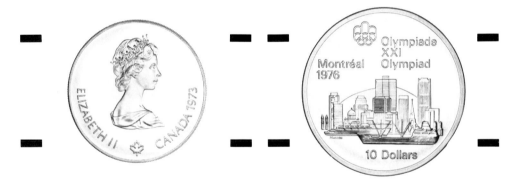

Silver 5- and 10-dollar Olympic coins, 1973-1976.

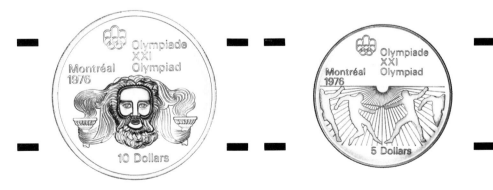

The silver coins were produced with two finishes, neither of which had previously been struck in such quantity by the Mint. The first finish was an attractive "satin" (frosted) effect which covered the entire coin. The second, or "proof" finish, provided a spectacular effect: frosted lettering and design set off against a brilliant mirror field. Special equipment had to be obtained for the production of these coins.

Even this growing number of products did not mark the end of the numismatic effort. The Mint was also becoming involved in the preparation of numismatic coins for its foreign customers. The first such order was placed by Jamaica late in 1971. This included $20 gold and $10 sterling silver coins. As the Mint's reputation grew, orders arrived quickly from the Cayman Islands, the Bahamas, Bermuda and the Isle of Man. The coins were as diverse as their geographical destinations. Denominations ranged from 25 pence for the Isle of Man to $100 for the Bahamas. The commemorative themes varied from the Queen's Silver Jubilee featured on coins for the Isle of Man, Bermuda and the Cayman Islands, to the tenth anniversary of Jamaica's independence.

But now a difficulty arose which threatened to interrupt this progress in foreign and numismatic coins. Domestic demand, recently so low as to encourage these new projects, suddenly began another dramatic increase. In 1973, production levels broke all previous records. The 821 million pieces struck exceeded by almost 40 million the 1968 total which had only been achieved with the assistance of the Philadelphia Mint.

The Mint benefited from six new presses but still lacked new premises. It could no longer hope to handle the demand if its activities continued to grow at their existing rapid pace. Although four new customers – Israel, Honduras, Barbados and Trinidad – were taken on in 1973, foreign coin orders had to be curtailed since existing contracts were to run for several years. There were other signs of a cutback: total production for foreign countries was down nearly 40 percent from 1972, and the Mint did not bid on a number of potential contracts.

The following year, this trend continued as domestic production surpassed one billion pieces. The total number of foreign coins produced showed a slight increase as existing contracts were honoured, but no new orders were accepted. Such a rejection of lucrative possibilities was a painful situation. Not everyone believed that this loss was unavoidable. The ultimate solution was a bold one – a new mint.

20

Notes:

1 The cost of the Games was over one
billion dollars, less than 10 percent
of which was covered by the sale
of Olympic coins.

2 The themes were I: Geographic,
II: Olympic Motifs, III: Early Canadian
Sports, IV: Olympic Track and Field
Sports, V: Olympic Summer Sports,
VI: Olympic Team and Body Contact
Sports, VII: Olympic Souvenirs.

The Winnipeg Plant

However successful the Mint had been in meeting coinage demands under the stress of changing conditions throughout the 1960s, it was clear that it could not do so indefinitely while confined to its original buildings. Already several functions had been given up, most importantly the melting and rolling of metals. As well, the striking of some ten-cent pieces had been contracted out to Philadelphia, and the Numismatic Division had been relocated to Hull.

The need for additional facilities had become abundantly clear. In fact this need had been recognized as early as the beginning of the decade. In November of 1960, the Master of the Mint had complained to the Finance Department about the difficulty of meeting coinage requests under the existing conditions. The Department of Public Works carried out improvements the following year, but only minor changes were made. It was obvious that, at the very least, major changes would soon have to be made.

The government was doubtful that even major renovations in the existing plant would be sufficient, and began to search for an alternative site for new premises. This search was carried out in the Ottawa area only. The Mint might have to abandon Sussex Drive, but the intention was to keep it in Ottawa.

" ... a new building specifically for the striking of coins."

Again and again during 1963 and 1964, the government suggested that construction of a new building would begin shortly. It was understood that the new facility would be operational within one or two years. But no ground was broken. Instead the government purchased supplies from outside sources and removed the Numismatic Division to help the Mint cope.

However the problem would not go away. A 1968 study into possible solutions described the Mint as "an antiquated plant." In fact funds were actually allocated for a new building, but still work was not begun.

The Mint's establishment as a Crown Corporation in 1969 made it much more likely that something would finally be done to relieve the pressure on the existing plant. However, in keeping with the earlier ironies of the Mint's history, no sooner was the Corporation ready to proceed then there was a marked decline in the country's need for coin. Even the first quarter of the year's business was actually only a carry-over from the heavy requirements of 1968. Soon instead of expanding, the Mint was reducing shifts and laying off casual employees. By the end of the year, a single shift was able to meet the demand with no temporary employees. It was hardly a favourable time for spending the $30 million allocated to build a new, high-capacity plant.

Nevertheless a search went on for suitable sites in the Ottawa area. Consideration was given to what character a new mint should have, and to the quality and costs of the most modern equipment. Several important questions had to be considered before construction could begin.

The first idea explored was the complete replacement of the Ottawa Plant. This would mean the reconstruction of all the departments, including the Melting and Rolling areas. But, by May of 1969, it was generally agreed that it would be better to keep the Ottawa plant for certain functions and design the new building specifically for the striking of coins. In particular, it would have no refinery and no melting area. Less than a year after the Mint's establishment as a Crown Corporation in February 1970, engineering consultants were engaged to design a new mint along these lines.

This increased the pressure to fix a location for the new mint. Although there had been some consideration given to a site outside of Ottawa – in 1963 Prime Minister Pearson had suggested Elliott Lake – there seemed little doubt that it would remain in the nation's capital. Certainly all sites given serious consideration during the preceding few years had been in the Ottawa area.

No binding decision had been taken however, and during the delay, new factors had arisen which placed Ottawa's claim in doubt. The government had recently adopted a policy of decentralizing its departments. This was now combined with a claim by Manitoba that the government make some restitution to it for the closure of a number of important military bases in the province.

In February 1970, Supply and Services Minister James Richardson, who was responsible to Parliament for the Mint, proposed that a study be conducted to assess the feasibility of locating the new plant in Winnipeg. Objections were quick to surface, and not only because Winnipeg happened to be the Minister's riding. It was claimed that the Mint was not like other government departments, many of which could just as easily be placed elsewhere. Besides it was legally stipulated that the country's coins had to be produced at a Mint in the National Capital Region.

More troublesome were the practical problems involved. It was one thing to divide the Mint in two; it was quite another to separate the two parts by over a thousand miles. It was anticipated that there would be difficulties in transferring staff and arranging for the supply of materials and for the distribution of coins. Nevertheless the study was undertaken. It maintained that the obstacles could be overcome and that such a division actually had merit. Notably Canada would be able to purchase its nickel strip conveniently from the Canadian firm of Sherritt-Gordon at Fort Saskatchewan in Alberta, rather than from its only competitor, the International Nickel Company of West Virginia.

While the majority of the arguments affecting the question were apparent at an early stage, they were not explored and defined in detail until nearly a year later, in early 1971. Cabinet approval for the recommendation was finally given in December of that year. At the time, there was no reason for anxiety over the delay. The Corporation's new ventures were only beginning to show results and the domestic demand, while rising, still remained below the crisis levels attained during the 1960s.

Construction of
Winnipeg Plant.

A Winnipeg site was acquired in June 1972. Construction began late in the year with completion scheduled for 1974. Progress during building gave little cause for worry. Planning for this mint had been much more thorough than for the first one in 1908. Numerous tests, studies and experiments had been conducted. Partly as a result of this intense preparation, construction went forward without major difficulties and stayed close to budgeted costs.

Despite this impressive building record and the slowed pursuit of foreign coin orders, there was nearly a crisis. The domestic coinage demand shot up during 1974, and again pushed the Mint to its limit. However the new facility was completed before serious difficulties arose.

The new plant is radically different from the Ottawa plant opened in 1908. Unlike its predecessor, the Winnipeg plant benefits from distinctively modern architecture and materials. It is designed to make the Mint's activities clear to visitors. Viewing galleries, complete with detailed explanations of each process, are carefully located throughout the plant. But the most important difference between the two plants lies in their facilities. Whereas the Ottawa plant, from its inception to the present, has featured all the expertise and machinery necessary to coinage design, engraving and production, the Winnipeg plant is clearly production-oriented. It has no means of producing alloys, receiving its coinage metals as blanks or strip from Ottawa or outside sources, and depends upon Ottawa for its punches. This plant concentrates on striking coins.

However limited this range may be in comparison with Ottawa's wide spectrum, it was precisely what was most needed in 1975. Early in that year, the new plant produced its first coins and relieved the uncomfortable pressure which had so often been felt by the Ottawa plant. By the end of 1975, the new plant was carrying one-third of the production load. It handled one-, five-, ten- and twenty-five-cent pieces. In 1976, the Winnipeg plant was officially opened. Its range extended into the large denomination coins, and its production increased to half of the country's needs.

" ... the Winnipeg plant is clearly production-oriented."

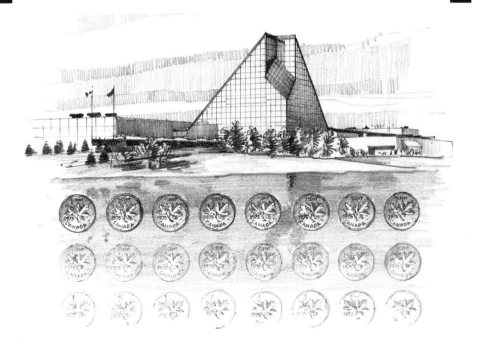

21

Steady Progress

With the Winnipeg plant in operation, Canada was again in a position to pursue contracts for producing foreign coinage. In the years immediately preceding its opening, the pressure of demands for domestic coinage had forced almost a complete curtailment of external business. By 1975, the clients required only 18 million pieces.

For a while full recovery was in doubt. Former clients might have found other suppliers, and there was no guarantee that new customers would be found as quickly as they had been earlier in the decade. In 1976, only one new client was added.

But during that year, the Marketing Division was established. The Mint soon acquired a global presence with its representatives travelling all over the world in pursuit of orders for foreign coinage. This strategy paid off: by the end of 1982, almost four billion coins had been struck for thirty-five foreign customers.

The importance of its international coinage business has provided several benefits for the Mint. Its income has been increased significantly in some years. The foreign contracts have also fostered a greater level of employment at the Mint than would otherwise have been possible. No less important has been the rich experience acquired by the Royal Canadian Mint's staff — experience in working with coinage designs, shapes and alloys not used for Canadian coins.

1979

Meeting with representative to discuss coinage designs.

Boxes of foreign coins ready for shipment.
Alan Carruthers.

Yvon Gariépy,
Master 1975-1981.

" ... a record output without undue strain."

Predictably no sooner was foreign business increasing strongly then the domestic demand rose. In 1978, a new record of almost 1.4 billion pieces was established. But this time, the resurgence did not interfere with the expanding foreign business. Even such great demands were still within the capacity of the Mint's facilities. It was now possible for the Mint to handle a record output without undue strain.

But there was a new challenge which increased production capacity could not resolve. The cost of copper and nickel had risen to the point where the Mint was losing money in the striking of the one- and five-cent pieces.

Focusing attention first on the cent, which accounted for nearly 60 percent of the domestic coin production in 1977, the Mint decided to reduce the size of the coin. In 1978, master tools were prepared for a 16 mm coin. The government was set to put the new-size cent into production when it was found that machines used by Toronto Transportation Commission could not discriminate the new one-cent coin from the aluminum token used for subways and buses. Public reaction was sufficient to prevent the introduction of any coinage modifications for the time being. Thus, at times during the next 18 months, our two smallest denominations were coined at a loss: the cent cost two cents and the five-cent piece cost six cents to produce.

Proposed reduced-diameter cent, 1978.

Bronze reduced thickness cent, 1980.

Bronze twelve-sided cent, 1983.

Bags of cents.
Telling (counting) machine and bags for shipment from Ottawa plant.
Murray Mosher.

"... a delight to behold."

It was not until 1980 that an alternative change was made: the cent was reduced in thickness (but not diameter), saving 13.6 percent on the amount of bronze required for each coin. The weight was reduced a further 10.7 percent in 1982 with the introduction of a 12-sided shape. In the same year, the 5-cent piece, formerly of pure nickel, was struck in the less expensive cupro-nickel (75 percent copper).

During this period, production of coins for domestic circulation continued with few major changes in the existing designs. Minor modifications were made from time to time and in 1979, the size of the Queen's portrait was altered slightly. It was made to occupy a fixed proportion of the coin diameter on all denominations.

The greatest design change involved the nickel dollar. In 1982, agreement was reached between Canada and Britain for the repatriation of the Dominion's Constitution. H.M. Queen Elizabeth II formally presented the Constitution to the Government of Canada in Ottawa, on April 17, 1982.

As a result of this historic event, 1982 production of the Voyageur nickel dollar was reduced and dies of a new design were put into the presses. The reverse featured a representation of Robert Harris' well-known painting of the Fathers of Confederation gathered at the conference table in Quebec City in 1864. The new coin was produced in large quantities and made readily available to the public through chartered banks.

Nickel commemorative dollar for the repatriation of Canada's Constitution, 1982.

Throughout the late 1970s and into the 1980s, the Mint's numismatic facility in Hull has maintained a steady course, largely independent of surges in circulating coinage demands.

The three different types of coin sets, introduced in 1971, continued to prove popular, as did the collectors' silver dollars. The latter quickly came to be as well-known for the novelty of their designs (which change every year) as for their workmanship.

The Mint introduced proof sets and coins for the first time in 1981. Proof coins are very high quality strikings, usually with frosted designs against a mirror-like field. It was not until 1973 that the Royal Canadian Mint obtained the necessary equipment for proof-coin production. However the only Canadian coins made available to the public in proof quality prior to 1981 were some of the coins for the Montreal Olympics and the $100 gold pieces. The new proof sets justly received wide acclaim: they are a delight to behold.

The highest denomination Canadian coin struck by the Hull Plant is the $100 gold piece, introduced in 1976 in connection with the Olympic program. The Olympic gold pieces, depicting an ancient Grecian athlete being honoured by the Goddess Athena, were available in 14 karat (K) gold 'Uncirculated' and 22 K 'Proof' editions.

All subsequent issues of the coin have been proof strikings, composed of 22 karats (.917) fine gold, containing one-half troy ounce of pure gold. Beginning in 1977, the alloying metal has been silver (instead of copper), which results in a colour much closer to that of pure gold. The $100 coin, like the silver dollar, receives a new design each year.

The production of numismatic coins has not been restricted to domestic issues. Year by year new countries request the Mint to produce collectors' coins for them. Orders from around the world have come from such countries as Fiji, Turks and Caicos, Panama and New Zealand. By the early 1980s, the Mint had more than thirty nations on its books.

Proof silver dollar, 1981.

Cayman Islands.
Silver "Six Queens" 50 dollars,
1976.

Highlights among the additions
in the sixties and early seventies were:
the Defries Medal for the Canadian
Public Health Association (1966);
medals for Photographic Excellence
for the National Film Board of Canada
(1967); and the Royal Canadian
Geographic Society's Massey Medal
(1973).

Among the medals struck for special
occasions rather than for annual presentation were the 5,000 Expo medals
in 1970, and the three medals struck
to commemorate the Duke of Edinburgh's
visit to the Mint in 1973.

Such work ensured that by 1976, when
the Winnipeg plant opened and relieved
the pressure on the Ottawa facilities,
the Medal section was broadly experienced and well respected. This was
the position which the Deputy Master,
J.H. Campbell, had envisioned
for it as early as 1926.

But success did not lead to compla-
cency. On the contrary, starting
in 1976, the Department went through
a period of development and diversification which rivalled that of any other
department in the Mint.

The coins display great variety: there
is an astonishing $2500 gold piece
for the Bahamas and the distinctive 'Six
Queens' commemoratives for the Cayman
Islands.

Not surprisingly, the Medal Section
of the Mint has recently experienced
growth similar to that of the other Mint
departments, particularly since 1975.
Until this date, the pattern established
in the fifties continued with very few
exceptions. Generally production
could be divided into large and small
orders. The former were placed chiefly
by the Department of Defence Production (more recently a part of Supply
and Services Canada) which distributed the Canadian Forces Decoration
Medals and the Department of Veterans
Affairs which handled the various Second World War stars. The Royal Canadian
Mounted Police and the Governor
General's Office also regularly ordered
significant numbers of a large variety
of medals. But by far the most numerous clients were those placing orders
for less than twenty medals. Most orders
were repeated year after year and were
joined each year by new orders just
as they had been in the fifties.

"... the Mint has become increasingly involved in other non-coinage sidelines:..."

Although there were notable additions to the small order category during the ensuing years, including the creation of the fine gold Canadian Coast Guard College Centennial Award in 1976, the most marked change occurred in the number of large orders. Pieces were struck for Consumer and Corporate Affairs, for Operation Sail 1976, for the Dominion of Canada Rifle Association and for the inauguration of the Winnipeg plant. But none surpassed in public interest the medals issued for the Olympics in Montreal. This growth in large orders continued throughout the late 1970s, with the medals for the Moscow Olympics, struck in 1979, marking a significant step into the world market.

In recent years, the Mint has become increasingly involved in other non-coinage sidelines: tokens (transit tokens, bridge tokens, toll-gate tokens, etc.) and trade dollars for such events as the Quebec Winter Carnival and the Calgary Stampede. By the end of 1982, the Mint had struck more than two million tokens and trade dollars. Their production has provided the Mint's staff, particularly the engravers, with additional useful experience.

Among the most satisfying of the success stories associated with the Royal Canadian Mint during the last few years is that of the Gold Maple Leaf programme.

During the 1950s, the Canadian Government altered its gold policy. Although it continued to receive most of the gold refined in Ottawa, it introduced in 1951 a policy which allowed mines to store their refined gold in the Mint for later return to them. This gold would in turn be exported or sold to Canadian processors.

Throughout the 1950s, the percentage of stored or "designated" gold rose. It often comprised as much as one-third of the total amount the Mint refined. This increasing diversion of gold from the government to the growing needs of industry reflected a worldwide competition for the precious metal between governments (often through their central banks) and private industry.

Gold Olympic Games (Montreal) medal, 1976.

Pouring a .9999 fine gold bar
in the Refinery,
Murray Mosher.

Finally in 1968, the leading banks of the world agreed not to add new gold output to the stocks already stored in their vaults. This made the metal more available for private consumption. The Royal Canadian Mint reacted to this development by improving the purity of gold it produced. Instead of .995 fine bars (an international monetary standard), it produced .9999 fine bars more suitable for manufacturing. The increased fineness was made possible by a two-stage refining process: chlorination to a fineness of about .995 followed by electrolytic treatment in an expanded, 48-cell plant.

Well before 1968, public interest in gold ownership had been growing. Coins were a convenient form in which to hold the metal. For the typical investor, the cost of the coins would be little more than the bullion value of the metal. Indeed, some countries like Austria, Mexico and Great Britain had recently been striking limited quantities of gold coins of long established denominations, for the purpose of serving the gold bullion coin investment market.

In 1967, the Government of South Africa brought the concept of the bullion coin to new levels when it introduced the Krugerrand, in order to boost sales of its gold. Each coin contains one Troy ounce of pure (fine) gold, present in the form of a gold-copper alloy (.917 fine). The official unit of currency in South Africa is the rand, and the value of the Krugerrand "coin" is not directly related to it.

Following the success of the Krugerrand, it was suggested in 1976 that Canada should enter the bullion coin market. The Canadian gold producers were particularly anxious to see such coins struck to help assure a brisk market for the country's gold. Finally in May 1978, Parliament approved an amendment to the Currency and Exchange Act, which allowed Cabinet to authorize the production of Canadian bullion gold coins.

"... it was suggested...that Canada should enter the bullion coin market."

1979

In February 1979, the government established the Gold Maple Leaf programme on a three-year trial basis. Product planning emphasized the need to offer a coin distinct from the Krugerrand and which would have a strong Canadian identity. It was decided that to meet these needs each coin would bear on its reverse a stunning likeness of a maple leaf. It would contain one ounce of pure (at least .999 fine) gold. Unlike the Krugerrand, no alloying metal would be added. Also unlike its South African rival, the Gold Maple Leaf would be a legal tender coin (face value $50) in the true currency of the issuing country. Finally the Mint determined that it would sell the Gold Maple Leaf coin for a few percent over the current value of the one Troy ounce of fine gold it contained.

By 1981, the Gold Maple Leaf programme had become so successful that parliamentary authorization was given for the coin's production on a continuing basis. Responding to a demand for gold bullion coins of smaller value, the government also authorized the striking of fractional Gold Maple Leaf coins from 1982 onward: a $1/4$ ounce coin (face value $10) and a $1/10$-ounce coin (face value $5).

Master Engraver Walter Ott at work on the model for the reverse of the Gold Maple Leaf $50 coin. Murray Mosher.

Master Engraver Walter Ott comparing the reverse punch for the Gold Maple Leaf $50 coin with the Mint artwork. Murray Mosher.

"...the government established the Gold Maple Leaf programme..."

One-tenth, one-quarter and one-ounce
Gold Maple Leaf coins,
1982.

" ... outstanding among the world's coin-producing facilities... "

Beginning with the 1982 fractional coins and continuing with the one-ounce coin in 1983, the Gold Maple Leaf coins are now guaranteed to contain gold of .9999 purity. Accordingly the maple leaf on each coin is flanked by "9999" instead of "999" on the earlier versions of the one-ounce coin. The Gold Maple Leaf programme's success is clear from the fact that, by the end of 1982, nearly four million ounces of gold had been sold in this way. Most of these coins, furthermore, are sold outside Canada, thereby aiding our balance of payments.

The story of the creation and success of the Gold Maple Leaf coin series brings this history back to where it began – to the modern Mint. Fifteen years ago, as a new Crown Corporation, the Mint was encouraged to seek new sources of revenue. It has done that admirably. Today it is outstanding among the world's coin-producing facilities for its diversity. It spans the globe with coins for distant nations, delights collectors with the excellence of its numismatic products, strikes medals in recognition of outstanding services and events, supplies tokens and trade dollars, and refines the precious metal with which to make the purest gold coins in the world. At the same time, the Royal Canadian Mint supplies its home country with an unprecedented number of circulating coins to a high standard of excellence. Indeed the Mint's future looks as bright as its past has been fascinating.

Appendix 1

CHIEF EXECUTIVE OFFICERS OF THE MINT 1908~1983

Deputy Masters
Royal Mint, Ottawa Branch

James Bonar	1908-1919
A.H.W. Cleave	1919-1925
J.H. Campbell	1925-1931

Masters
Royal Canadian Mint

J.H. Campbell	1931-1937
H.E. Ewart	1938-1944
Position vacant	1945-1946
A.P. Williams (Mint Secretary, Acting Master)	1946-1947
W.C. Ronson	1947-1953
A.P. Williams	1954-1959
N.A. Parker	1959-1968
E.F. Brown (Acting Master)	1968-1970
G.W. Hunter	1970-1975
Yvon Gariépy	1975-1981
D.M. Cudahy (Acting Master)	1981-1982
J.C. Corkery	1982-

Appendix 2

CANADIAN COMMEMORATIVE COINS, 1935~1983

Date	Denomination	Subject Commemorated
1935	$1	25th anniversary of the accession of King George V.
1939	$1	Visit of King George VI, Queen Elizabeth and Princesses Elizabeth and Margaret to Canada in 1939.
1949	$1	Entry of Newfoundland into Confederation in 1949.
1951	5¢	Isolation of nickel in 1751.
1958	$1	Western gold rush and the establishment of British Columbia as a British Crown colony in 1858.
1964	$1	The 1864 meetings in Charlottetown, P.E.I. and Quebec City, P.Q., which paved the way for Confederation.
1967	1, 5, 10, 25, 50¢ $1, $20	Confederation in 1867 of the provinces of Canada, New Brunswick and Nova Scotia to form the Dominion of Canada.
1970	$1	Entry of Manitoba into Confederation in 1870.
1971	$1 (nickel), $1 (silver)	Entry of British Columbia into Confederation in 1871.
1973	$1 (nickel)	Entry of Prince Edward Island into Confederation in 1873.
1973	25¢, $1 (silver)	Formation of the North West Mounted Police (later the R.C.M.P.) in 1873.
1974	$1 (nickel), $1 (silver)	Founding of the City of Winnipeg in 1874.
1975	$1 (silver)	Founding of the City of Calgary in 1875.
1973-76	$5 and $10 (seven designs each), $100 (two finenesses)	Staging of the Olympic Games in Montreal in 1976.
1976	$1 (silver)	Opening of the Library of Parliament in 1876.

1977	$1 (silver), $100	25th anniversary of the accession of Queen Elizabeth II.
1978	$1 (silver)	Staging of the 11th Commonwealth Games in Edmonton in 1978.
1978	$100	Canadian unity.
1979	$1 (silver)	The first voyage by a commercial ship on the Great Lakes in 1679.
1979	$100	International Year of the Child.
1980	$1 (silver), $100	Transfer in 1880 of the Arctic Islands from British to Canadian control.
1981	$1 (silver)	Authorization of the transcontinental railway in 1881.
1981	$100	Adoption of "O Canada" as our national anthem.
1982	$1 (nickel), $100	Patriation of Canada's constitution in 1982.
1982	$1 (silver)	Founding of the City of Regina in 1882.
1983	$1 (silver)	University Games, Edmonton.
1983	$100	Landing of Sir Humphrey in St. John's, Newfoundland in 1583 and the establishment of Newfoundland as the first British colony in the New World.

Appendix 3

DESIGNERS, ENGRAVERS, AND MODELLERS OF CANADIAN COINAGE 1858~1983

PROVINCE OF CANADA: 1, 5, 10, 20¢   1858-1859

All denominations were designed and engraved by L.C. Wyon.

NEW BRUNSWICK: ½, 1, 5, 10, 20¢   1861-1864

The obverses employed existing portraits by L.C. Wyon; the ½ and 1¢ used British Imperial farthing and ½d tools. The ½ and 1¢ reverses were engraved by L.C. Wyon from a wreath model by C. Hill. The Canadian reverse punches were used for the 5 & 10¢, but the 20¢ reverse was new, possibly the work of G.W. Wyon.

NOVA SCOTIA: ½, 1¢,   1861-1864

Both denominations were as for the New Brunswick ½ and 1¢ above.

NEWFOUNDLAND
VICTORIA COINAGE: 1, 5, 10, 20, 50¢, $2   1865-1900

The portraits are the work of L.C. Wyon. The 1¢ reverse and probably the 1¢ obverse lettering are by T.J. Minton. The silver reverses were engraved by L.C. Wyon, probably after designs by Horace Morehen. The $2 reverse was by L.C. Wyon.

EDWARD VII COINAGE: 1, 5, 10, 20, 50¢   1903-1910

The obverses employ a portrait modelled by G.W. DeSaulles. The 5 & 10¢ reverses were by DeSaulles, but similar designs for the 20 & 50¢ were engraved by W.H.J. Blakemore after DeSaulles' death. The 1¢ reverse was a modification by Blakemore of the previous Minton design.

GEORGE V: 1, 5, 10, 20, 25, 50¢   1911-1936

The obverse portrait was modelled by Sir E.B. MacKennal. The 25¢ reverse was by W.H.J. Blakemore, modifying the 20¢ reverse; the other reverses continue from the previous reign.

GEORGE VI: 1, 5, 10¢   1938-1947

The obverses were based on a portrait model by Percy Metcalfe. The cent reverse was designed and engraved by Walter J. Newman. The other reverses were carried over from the previous reign.

PRINCE EDWARD ISLAND: 1¢   1871

L.C. Wyon engraved the obverse, using a portrait model by William Theed. The reverse was also Wyon's work.

DOMINION OF CANADA

The situation is complicated by the fact that slight changes were made from time to time in long-running designs. Some merely represented alteration of existing punches or fresh reductions from existing models; however, others were copies, sometimes by individuals who did not engrave the original designs. Except for *gross* differences, only the principal varieties are noted here.

VICTORIA: 1, 5, 10, 25, 50¢   1870-1901

1, 25 & 50¢ obverses; designed and engraved by L.C. Wyon, using a portrait model by William Theed.

1¢ reverse, 5 & 10¢ obverses and reverses: utilized punches prepared for the Province of Canada. The "small leaves" 1¢ reverse, introduced in 1891, was probably the work of G.W. DeSaulles.

25 & 50¢ reverses: designed and engraved by L.C. Wyon.

EDWARD VII: 1, 5, 10, 25, 50¢   1902-1910

Obverses: designed and engraved by G.W. DeSaulles
Reverses: initial varieties were by DeSaulles; new 5¢ (1903) and 10¢ (1909)
wreaths were probably by W.H.J. Blakemore.

GEORGE V: 1, 5, 10, 25, 50¢ – $1., $5., $10   1911-1936

Obverses: from a portrait model by Sir E.B. MacKennal, except for the 1935 $1 portrait which was the work of Percy Metcalfe.

Reverses: 1¢ (large) – a new engraving by W.H.J. Blakemore
1¢ (small) – designed by Fred Lewis; engraved by W.H.J. Blakemore.
5¢ (silver), 10¢ ("large leaves"), 25¢, 50¢ – carried over from the previous reign.
5¢ (nickel) – designed and engraved by W.H.J. Blakemore.
10¢ ("small leaves") – engraved by W.H.J. Blakemore.
$1 – 1935-36 – designed and modelled by Emanuel Hahn.
$5 & $10 – designed and engraved by W.H.J. Blakemore.

GEORGE VI: 1, 5, 10, 25, 50¢ – $1.   1937-1952

Obverses: from a portrait model by T.H. Paget.

Reverses: 1¢, 5¢, 50¢ – designed by G.E. Kruger-Gray
10¢ & 25¢ – designed and modelled by Emanuel Hahn.
$1 ("voyageur") carried over from previous reign.
5¢ ("victory" 1942-45) – designed and engraved by Thomas Shingles.
5¢ ("refinery" 1951) – designed by Stephen Trenka; modelled by Thomas Shingles.
$1 – 1949 – designed and engraved by Thomas Shingles.

ELIZABETH II: 1, 5, 10, 25, 50¢, $1, $5, $10; $20, $50, $100

Obverses: 1953-64 – from a portrait model by Mrs. Mary Gillick.
1965 on – from a portrait model by Arnold Machin.

Reverses: 1, 5, 10, 25¢ – 1953-66, 1968 on
50¢ –   1953-54   Based on the original
$1 ("voyageur")   models from the previous reign
50¢ – 1955-58 – New engraving by Thomas Shingles.
50¢ – 1959-66 – 1968 on – designed by Thomas Shingles.
$1 – 1958 – designed by Stephen Trenka; modelled by Thomas Shingles.
$1 – 1964 – designed by Dinko Vodanovic; modelled by Thomas Shingles.
1¢ to $1 – 1967 – designed by Alex Colville.

DENOMINATION & DATE	DESIGNER(S)	MODELLER(S)
$1 nickel 1970	Raymond Taylor	Walter Ott
$1 nickel 1971	Thomas Shingles	Thomas Shingles
$1 silver 1971	Patrick Brindley	Walter Ott
25¢ 1973	Paul Cederberg	Patrick Brindley
$1 silver 1973	Paul Cederberg	Ago Aarand & Patrick Brindley
$1 nickel 1973	Terry Manning	Walter Ott
$1 nickel & silver 1974	Paul Pederson	Walter Ott
$1 silver 1975	Donald D. Paterson	Walter Ott
$1 silver 1976	Ago Aarand & Patrick Brindley	Walter Ott
$1 silver 1977	RCM Staff	Ago Aarand
$100 gold 1977	Raymond Lee	Walter Ott
$1 silver 1978	Raymond Taylor	
$100 gold 1978	Roger Savage	Ago Aarand
$1 silver 1979	Walter Schleup	Terrance Smith
$100 gold 1979	Carola Tietz	Victor Coté
$1 silver 1980	Donald D. Paterson	Walter Ott
$100 gold 1980	Arnoldo Marchetti	Sheldon Beveridge
$1 silver 1981	Christopher Gorey	Ago Aarand
$100 gold 1981	Roger Savage	Sheldon Beveridge & Walter Ott
$1 nickel "Constitution" 1982	RCM Staff	Ago Aarand
$1 silver 1982	Huntley Brown	Sheldon Beveridge
$100 gold 1982	Friedrich Peter	Walter Ott
$1 silver 1983	Carola Tietz	Victor Coté
$100 gold 1983	John Jaciw	Ago Aarand

OLYMPIC COINS

$5 World Map 1973	Georges Huel	
$5 Kingston & Sailboats 1973	Georges Huel	Terrance Smith
$10 World Map 1973	Georges Huel	
$10 Montreal and Ship 1973	Georges Huel	Ago Aarand
$5 Athlete & Torch 1974	Anthony Mann	Patrick Brindley
$5 Olympic Rings 1974	Anthony Mann	Walter Ott
$10 Head of Zeus 1974	Anthony Mann	Patrick Brindley & Sheldon Beveridge
$10 Temple Zeus 1974	Anthony Mann	Walter Ott
$5 Canoeing 1974	Ken Danby	Patrick Brindley & Sheldon Beveridge
$5 Rowing 1974	Ken Danby	Terrance Smith
$10 Lacrosse 1974	Ken Danby	Walter Ott
$10 Cycling 1974	Ken Danby	Ago Aarand
$5 Marathon 1975	Leo Yerxa	Walter Ott
$5 Women's Javelin 1975	Leo Yerxa	Walter Ott
$10 Men's Hurdles 1975	Leo Yerxa	Patrick Brindley
$10 Women's Shot Put 1975	Leo Yerxa	Patrick Brindley
$5 Diving 1975	Linda Cooper	
$5 Swimming 1975	Linda Cooper	
$10 Paddling 1975	Linda Cooper	
$10 Sailing 1975	Linda Cooper	
$5 Fencing 1976	Shigeo Fudula	
$5 Boxing 1976	Shigeo Fudula	
$10 Field Hockey 1976	Shigeo Fudula	
$10 Soccer 1976	Shigeo Fudula	
$5 Olympic Village 1976	Elliott Morrison	Sheldon Beveridge
$5 Olympic Flame 1976	Elliott Morrison	Walter Ott
$10 Olympic Stadium 1976	Elliott Morrison	Ago Aarand
$10 Olympic Velodrome 1976	Elliott Morrison	Terrance Smith
$100 Athena & Athlete 1976	dora de Pedery-HUNT	dora de Pedery-HUNT and Walter Ott

BULLION COINS

$5 gold 1/10 Troy ounce 1982 on	RCM Staff	RCM Staff
$10 gold 1/4 Troy ounce 1982 on	RCM Staff	RCM Staff
$50 gold 1 Troy ounce 1979 on	RCM Staff	RCM Staff

Appendix 4

CANADIAN NUMISMATIC COIN PRODUCTION AT THE MINT 1908~1983

Numismatic coins are, by their very nature, special. They are not for general circulation but are to be distributed to collectors or used for presentation purposes. Such coins, consequently, are produced with greater care than usual and typically have surfaces which are superior to those on coins made for circulation. The superior surfaces are the result of some or all of the following: (a) extra polishing of the blanks, (b) the use of selected or specially polished dies, (c) greater effective striking force, through a single, heavy blow or multiple blows (circulation coins are struck only once).

Over the years, the finish on Canadian numismatic coins has varied. The pre1937 issues have an overall frosted or "satin" appearance. It is more "glittering" and more uniform than on corresponding circulation strikes, and the design details are more sharply defined. A modern example approximating this finish can be found on the "Uncirculated" version of the 1973-76 $5 and $10 Canadian Olympic coins. On some 1937 and most of the 1938 to mid-1940s issues, the raised design elements are frosted, but the background (field) is brilliant. This creates a beautiful two-tone effect reminiscent of the Specimen coins of the Victorian era. The two-tone finish recently has been brought to perfection on the Proof versions of the 1973-76 Olympic coins, the 1981 and later Proof sets and on the $100 gold coins.

The third finish is brilliant overall. It first made its appearance on Specimen coins of the last half of the 1940s. By 1950, this finish was so brilliant that the coins themselves looked as though they had been individually polished. A similar finish has been employed for the numismatic coins of 1970-80 and the Uncirculated and Specimen sets of 1981 to date.

A considerably less brilliant version of the monotone finish is seen on the numismatic issues of 1953-69. The early satin-finish numismatic coins were officially designated "Specimen" coins. Their production began in 1908, the first year of the Ottawa Mint's operation. During the year, some 1000 cased sets of Specimen one-through fifty-cent pieces were struck. A small coinage of 636 goild sovereigns, produced in December, is also believed to have been of Specimen quality, even though most of it was issued for general circulation. issued for general circulation.

Very little numismatic activity seems subsequently to have taken place until late in 1911. Production of numismatic one-through fifty-cent pieces and gold sovereigns for the new monarch, George V, then began. This minting activity continued into the following year for the silver and bronze and in the spring was supplemented with $5 and $10 gold pieces. During 1912, two types of cased numismatic sets were offered: a silver and bronze set, dated 1911 and an expanded set containing the 1911 silver and bronze denominations, a 1911 sovereign and 1912 $5 and $10 gold pieces.

Between 1913 and 1936, numismatic coins were usually produced in very small quantities and were probably not generally available for purchase by the public. Few people knew of their existence. Routine mintages were undoubtedly fewer than twenty sets per year; it is possible that none was struck for some years in the teens. Exceptions to the low mintage role occurred in 1922 for the new nickel five-cent piece and in 1935 for the commemorative silver dollar.

The Royal Canadian Mint expanded its Specimen coin production in 1937 to mark the issue of new designs for King George VI. A satin-finish set of the new coins was sold to the public through the Bank of Canada. In addition, dies with highly-polished fields were used to strike a small number of "two-tone" sets reserved for presentation and not sold to the public.

As collector interest in Canadian coins increased after World War II, mail inquiries for coin sets began to come to the Mint. At first, they were handed over to the Bank of Canada, which assembled the required year sets. In 1949, the Mint began to put aside sets of coin for sale to collectors. Their assembly and issue were handled by Mint Office staff and took place on a very small scale. By 1952, the Royal Canadian Mint had established a separate Numismatic Section. The Bank of Canada then ceased distributing coins to collectors.

The Mint's Numismatic Section consisted of one man, working in a small office. His main function at first was to maintain a stock of circulation coins to satisfy public requests for year sets. It was possible to obtain sets of the current year, as well as any set dated back to 1949.

Late in 1953, the Mint decided to upgrade the quality of coins it offered to collectors. A small number of "Special" sets of 1953 coins were produced and distributed in the fall of that year. These coins, while clearly superior to circulation coins, did not possess a finish as good as Specimen coins used for presentation. By year-end, an additional 1200 "Special" sets of 1953 coins had come off the presses and had been turned over to the Numismatic Section.

The production of "Special" coin, as the Mint referred to it internally, actually began in 1949. In that year, the silver dollar was a commemorative piece for the entry of Newfoundland into Confederation. It was decided to strike and package this coin with particular care. Dies were retired sooner than usual. Most coins were packed in cardboard or plastic tubes (instead of loose in canvas bags) for issue. Small numbers of 1950, 1951, and 1952 coins (particularly dollars) were of "Special" quality.

The Mint chose to label publicly as "Uncirculated" all coins that were not of Specimen quality. Understandably this was not good enough for the numismatic trade. The "Special" coin was soon designated "Proof-like" by a Toronto coin dealer, and this term eventually became widely accepted. It was never adopted by the Mint, which has continued to use "Uncirculated".

Meanwhile small quantities of Specimen coins continued to be struck. At the end of 1952 and again in 1953, residual stocks of Specimen coins were mixed with the other qualities of coins being sold. Thus some 1949 to 1953 sets which collectors received from the Mint were partly or entirely made up of "Proof-like" or Specimen coin.

Between 1954 and 1970, the only numismatic sets routinely offered to the public were "Uncirculated" six-coin year sets. At first, each was housed in a piece of white cardboard covered with cellophane, but this was replaced by a flat, clear polyester pouch from 1961 onward.

In 1970, the Mint began the expansion of its numismatic product line. A limited quantity of Specimen coin sets of a higher quality than the standard "Uncirculated" were prepared. Most were delivered to Prime Minister Trudeau for presentation during the trip he made to Japan that year. Each set was housed in a narrow, leather-covered case. These sets also were shown to collectors at major numismatic shows that year for the purpose of ascertaining the extent of public interest in improved-quality numismatic products.

The major difference between the new sets and the "Uncirculated" sets was that the former were double-struck, whereas the latter were struck only once. The coins in both types of set were given a brilliant, polished finish which would be the standard for the next ten years.

Although small numbers of the double-struck 1970 sets were sold to the public, it was not until 1971 that the two kinds of collector's coin were widely offered. Three types of set could be purchased. The "Regular" set was the continuation of the singly-struck coins in a polyester film pouch. A "Custom" set, housed in a square, vinyl-covered case, could also be purchased. It was a seven-coin set, with an extra cent to show the obverse side. Initially the coins were singly-struck. The seven-coin "Prestige" set, with its two $1 coins, was the finest set available to the public. All coins were double-struck and housed in a leather-covered rectangular case. In 1971 and 1972, both dollars were nickel; from 1973 to 1980, one was nickel and the other was silver. In 1977, the production of singly-struck numismatic coin ceased and all three sets received the same quality double-struck coins.

In addition to sets, the Mint also gave special attention to the silver dollars, popular with collectors since their introduction in 1935. In some years, numismatic-quality dollars were offered separately, so it was not necessary to purchase an entire year set to obtain them. To fill the gap left by converting the circulating dollar from a silver coin to a smaller nickel version in 1968, the Mint re-introduced the silver dollar in 1971. This new coin is strictly for collectors and, like the $100 gold pieces, has no circulating counterpart.

The year 1981 saw further important changes in the Mint's numismatic products. The "Custom" set was replaced by a six-coin "Specimen" set containing a nickel dollar but lacking a silver dollar. Each coin is housed in a clear plastic capsule, mounted in a blue, rectangular plastic case. The coins continue to display the previous brilliant polished finish.

The most striking change was in the double-dollar set: in place of the "Prestige" set, a seven-coin "Proof" set was offered. Proofs are the ultimate in quality and appearance. The frosted raised design elements are set off against a very highly-polished field. Previous production of Canadian Proof coins had been restricted to the Olympic Proof coinage of 1973-76 and the $100 series form 1977 to date.

Thus the Royal Canadian Mint has produced coins for collectors throughout its existence. Its ability to produce such coins gradually improved to the point that today, the Mint's numismatic products compare favourably with any in the world.

Index I

A

Aarand, Ago, 261, 262
'A MARI USQUE AD MARE' on 1927
Confederation medal, 127
on 1939 Royal Visit medal, 161

Alloys, coinage, 19
defined, 6
bronze, 44, 115, 168, 171
cupro-nickel, 2, 6
gold, 6
silver, 119, 168, 216, 217

Annealing, defined, 8
of blanks, 8, 196

Arctic islands, $1 and $100 commemorative coins for (1980), 260

Athena (Greek goddess) on 1976 gold
$100 coins, 247

Assay office, mentioned, 67
Vancouver, 82
opened, 67

Assay Dept., 83, 84, 92

Austria, 250

Australia, 202

B

'Bag marks', 190

Bank of Canada,
holds $5 and $10 gold coinage
of 1912-14, 102
mentioned, 135
sells 1937 specimen sets to the
public, 152, 270

Bars, coinage, 194, 195
gold, 103, 104
medal, 182

'Beaver', Canadian (proposed gold coin),
85

Bennett, R.B., visits England (1930),
132
reads bill creating the Royal Canadian
Mint (1931), 132
decides Canada is to have silver
dollar, 139
proposes superimposed heads of King
and Queen for new dollar, 140
releases details of new dollar, 141

Beveridge, Sheldon, 266, 267

Bimetallism:
in Great Britain, 32, 34

Blakemore, W.H.J., 258-260

Blanks, coinage, 5, 166, 168, 176,
194, 207, 221, 240, 269
defined, 5
defective, 7, 115, 195
foreign, produced in Ottawa, 110,
227
nickel, produced in the U.S., 120

Bluenose (ship), as model for the 'fishing
schooner' ten cents, 151

Bonar, Dr. James, appointed first Deputy
Master of the Ottawa Mint, 70
worries about opening date for Mint,
71
mentioned, 74, 91, 93, 105, 129
opposes internal changes in Mint, 76
questions necessity for gold coinage,
82
stresses need to accept all gold
shipments, 84
endeavours to obtain designs
for domestic gold coinage, 85
bemoans inability to produce master
tools in Ottawa, 91, 202
promises Dept. of Finance that sovereigns will soon be delivered, 92

D

Danby, Ken, 267

Dawson, mentioned, 64

Defense Production, Dept. of, 248

De Meulles, Jacques, invents French
Regime *card money*, 30

De Pedery-HUNT, dora, 267

'DEI GRATIA'', 94, 95, 99, 140, 211

Delamarre, Raymond, 127

Deputy Masters, Royal Mint, Ottawa,
257

DeSaulles, G.W., 263-64

Designers of Canadian coins, 263-67

Die axis arrangements, 154, 164

Dies, coinage, 5, 8, 269
defined, 5
chromium plating of, 14, 170-197
production of, 14, 197, 208

Dobson, Frank, 149

Dollar, Canadian, devaluation of (1962),
226

Dollar, circulating silver:
commemorative (1935), 139-41,
143, 160, 259, 265
1936, 143, 265
1937, 154, 265
commemorative (1939), 157-58,
160-61, 205, 259, 265
suspension of, coinage of, during World
War II, 171
commemorative (1949), 190, 192,
259, 265
commemorative (1958), 204, 259,
265

commemorative (1964), 210, 259,
265
cessation of coinage of (1967), 219,
229

Dollar, circulating nickel:
first coinage of (1968), 215, 219-20
commemorative (1970), 231, 259,
266
commemorative (1971), 229-31,
259, 266
Voyageur (1972), 230
commemorative (1973), 230, 259,
266
commemorative (1974), 230, 250,
266
Voyageur and commemorative (1982),
246, 250, 266

Dollar, .500 fine silver numismatic:
first coinage of (1971), 229-30, 259,
266
Voyageur (1972), 230
commemorative (1973), 230, 259,
266
commemorative (1974), 230, 259,
266
commemorative (1975), 230, 259,
266

Dollar, 'holey', of Prince Edward Island,
32

Dollars, 'trade', 24, 249, 254

Dollars, Spanish (-American), 27, 32-33

'Doubloons', 27

Doughty, Dr. Arthur, 85, 141

Douglas, James, 42-43

Drawings for coinage, 9, 86-87, 96, 98,
120, 126-27, 141-42, 150-52, 158,
172, 174

Drayton, Sir Henry, 120

refining of:
    by chlorination, 19, 92, 103, 105,
    250
    by electrolysis, 19, 83-84, 92-93
    250
    'rough', 83-84, 93, 100, 103
    rush, B.C., 42
    Klondike (Yukon), 58, 63-64, 67
    South African, sent to Ottawa
    for refining, 107, 110, 135, 250

Gordon, Walter, 227

Gorey, Christopher, 261

Gossett, Capt. D., 42-43

Great Britain, 202, 250

Grey, Countess of, 73

Grey, Earl, 73

Griffon (ship), sails on the Great Lakes,
    $1 commemorative coin for (1979),
    260, 266

Guinea, British, 31

H

Hahn, Emanuel, commissioned to design
    dollar reverse (1934), 141
    works on designs for 1937 coinage,
    151-52
    certain designs selected for 1937
    coinage, 150-51
    commissioned to model dollar reverse
    (1938), 160
    identified as designer of the 1939
    commemorative dollar, reverse, 160
    commissioned to model Royal Visit
    medal reverse (1938), 161
    works on model for Royal Visit medal
    reverse, 162

Hahn, Gustav, wins design competition
    for cent (1927), 126

Halfpence, British, 31-32
    shortage of in British North America,
    32

Halfpenny, Copper Company of Upper
    Canada, 32

Halifax currency, 33

Harris, Robert, 246

Heaton's Mint, 41, 49

Hill, C, 258

Hincks, Sir Francis, 47

Hudson's Bay Co., 31, 42

Huel, Georges, 267

Hunter, G.W., 224, 257

I

'IND: IMP:', 187

India, independence of, 187

'INDIAE IMPERATOR', 187

Interior, Dept. of, 67

International Nickel Co., 198, 239

International Year of the Child, $100
    commemorative coin for (1979), 260,
    266

J

Jaciw, John, 261

Janvier machine, 196

Japan, 271

Johnson, Col. R.A., visits Ottawa Mint
    (1923), 129
    expresses opinions regarding design
    for the 1935 dollar, 140-41

aids in acquiring designs for 1937
coinage, 149
suggests changing die axis arrangement for Canadian coins, 154

K

King, W.L. Mackenzie, mentioned, 130
considers designs for 1937 coinage,
149
suggests use of "1" in denomination
of 1939 dollar, 158
suggests map for reverse of 1939
Royal Visit medal, 161
receives set of Royal Visit medals,
163

Kruger-Gray, G.E., invited to submit
designs for 1937 coinage, 149
certain designs selected for 1936
coinage, 150-52
mentioned, 149

Krugerrand, gold, 250, 252

L

Larkin, P.C., 130

Laurier, Sir Wilfrid, 58, 94

Lee, Raymond, 261

Lemaire, E.J., 141

Lewis, Fred, 118

Library of Parliament, building of,
$1 commemorative coin for (1976),
259, 266

Louis (French gold coins), 29

M

Macdonald, Sir John A., 45, 57

MacDonald, J.A.H., 126

Machin, Arnold, 211

Machine Dept., 197

MacKennal, Sir E.B., 140

Manitoba joins Confederation, $1 com-
memorative coin for (1970), 231,
259

Mann, Anthony, 267

Manning, Terry 266

Maple leaf, gold, 22, 250-54

Marchetti, Arnoldo, 266

Margaret Rose, Princess, 163

Master, Royal Canadian Mint, list of, 257

Matrix, reduction, 12

Matrices, production of, 12, 14

Matthew (ship), 190

Maunder, Ernest, 190

McInnes, T.R., 55, 57-58, 133

McInnes, W.W.B., 58, 64

Medal, Art Director's Club, 205
Canada, 180
Canadian Coast Guard College
Centennial, 249
Canadian Efficiency, 180
Canadian Forces Decoration, 248
Canadian Volunteer Service, 182,
185
Chemical Institute of Canada, 206
Confederation Commemorative
(1927), 127-28, 162
Coronation, Elizabeth II, 205
Defence of Britain, 185
Defries, 248
Duke of Edinburgh's Visit to the Mint
(1973), 248
Engineering Institute, 179, 205

N

Punches, coinage, 13-14, 96, 100,
157, 187, 240
production of, 13-14

Pyx, Trial of the, 91, 100

R

Reducing Machine, 11-12, 196

Refinery, Ottawa Mint:
addition to (1914), 103-04
additional building (1916), 107-08,
135
construction of first, 82-83, 89, 92
operation of, 92-93, 103-04, 111
regulations, 83, 103-04
Royal Canadian Mint, 19, 135-39,
249-50
new (1935), 180

Regina, founding of, $1 commemorative
coin for (1982), 260, 266

Remedy, fineness, 91
weight, 91

Rhodes, Edgar N., 141

Richardson, James, 239

Rigg, Edward, 91

Robb, J.A., 130, 132

Roberts, B.J., 141

Roe, John, 115

Rolling Department, 221

Ronson, W.C., 191, 257

Roosevelt, President, 163

Rose, Sir John, 49, 51

Royal Bank of Canada, 156

Royal Canadian Mint, expansion
of (1950), 194-97
head office, Vanier, 14

Hull plant, 2, 22, 247
Ottawa plant, 2, 8, 248
Winnipeg plant, 2, 4, 8, 16-18,
230-41, 243, 248-49

Royal Mint Advisory Committee, 202,
205

Royal Mint (London), 32, 37, 39, 49,
52, 62, 66, 68, 70, 75, 76, 82, 91,
93, 95, 105, 111, 122-23, 129,
139, 147, 149, 154, 157, 162-63,
168, 189-90, 202, 211

Royal Mint, Melbourne Branch, 66, 83
Ottawa Branch
choice of site for, 65-68
construction of, 67-68, 70
transfer to Canadian control, 123,
129-30, 132-33
Sydney Branch, 103, 129

Royal Visit, $1 commemorative coin and
medals for (1939), 157-64, 179,
201, 205, 250, 259, 265

S

Savage, Roger, 266

Schleup, Walter, 266

Scissel, 7

Scott, Barbara Ann, 205

Seigniorage, 1, 56, 119

Sherritt-Gordon, 239

Shillings, British, 31, 38

Shingles, Thomas, engraves reverse and
initial obverse for 1939 school children's medal, 162, 164
joins staff at the Royal Canadian Mint
(1939), 162, 174
works on five-cent piece designs and
master tools (1942-43), 174

T